Omar Sharif's Life in Bridge

Omar Sharif's Life in Bridge

Translated and adapted by

TERENCE REESE

First published in French, as Ma Vie au Bridge,
by Librairie Arthème Fayard, Paris, in 1982
This English translation first published in Great Britain in 1983
by Faber and Faber Limited
3 Queen Square, London WC1N 3AU
Filmset by Wilmaset, Birkenhead
Printed in Great Britain by
Redwood Burn Ltd., Trowbridge

British Library Cataloguing in Publication Data

Sharif, Omar
Omar Sharif's life in bridge.
1. Sharif, Omar 2. Contract bridge—Biography
I. Title II. Reese, Terence III. Ma vie au bridge. *English*
795.41'5'0924 GV1282.26.S/

ISBN 0-571-13098-4

Library of Congress Cataloging in Publication Data

Sharif, Omar, 1932–
Omar Sharif's Life in bridge.
Translation of: Ma vie au bridge.
1. Contract bridge. I. Title.
II. Title: Life in bridge.

GV1282.3.S42713 1983 795.41'5 82-25147
ISBN 0-571-13098-4 (pbk)

Contents

Early Days in Egypt

I

There was a time when in my innocence I believed that an actor—especially a film actor—pursued a life of devoted, unremitting toil; work as enthralling as that of the architect who built the pyramids, as interminable as that of the peasant who, beneath a burning sun, turns his waterwheel to fertilize the parched earth beside the Nile.

I was quite wrong. The principal work of an actor consists of—waiting. It's like crossing a desert where there is no detail to distract the mind or the eye. Sunlight is regulated by the electricians. The machinists, decorators, script-girls, and the rest of the team, perform their functions under the eye of the director, while you, the actor, find yourself ignored. You sit, yawning, in your chair with its canvas back, you chat with a colleague, a cigarette in your hand, or perhaps you do nothing, think of nothing. Suddenly the assistant director calls: 'Take your places, please!'

At once you are a different man—perhaps the one who has crossed a desert and found an oasis. You leap on to the more—or less—artificial scene, you concentrate fiercely, and you hear the famous CLAP, followed by the equally famous: 'Action!'

And for two or three minutes you perform a tiny portion of a scene which may or may not one day find a place in an important sequence of which you know neither the beginning nor the end.

Making a film is the most tedious business in the world. Let me say at once that the object of this book is to excite a passion for bridge, not for acting. In case you have any ambitions of that sort, bear in mind that the principal function of an actor is not to present himself as the world's sexiest man but to alter his entire personality as soon as the camera turns. He must be completely in his new character, ignoring altogether the strange surroundings, the lights, the technicians perched in uncomfortable and unlikely spots.

You are given no time to marshal your concentration. All your normal personality and characteristics must be forgotten. For a few minutes you are someone entirely new, then you sink back into hours of tedious waiting. It is an existence that makes you desperate for a new, consuming interest.

I was twenty when I made my first film. It was directed by a friend who, like myself, was a Lebanese Christian living in Egypt. I played opposite the great star, Faten Hamamam, who later became my wife. And, as I have just explained, I often sat about for two or three hours before playing my part of a young man who triumphs over love and death.

During these hours of waiting it wasn't possible to read serious literature, only light novels. I see myself again in a small library in the centre of Alexandria, looking for books that would be amusing but not silly. I had read *Anna Karenina* and most of the other Russian romances. I wasn't in the mood for Proust, who later gave me enormous pleasure, nor for Thackeray, although I had very much enjoyed *Vanity Fair* and had felt I would like to play his hero, Pendennis. Then, one day, my eyes alighted on Charles Goren's *Better Bridge for Better Players*. I still recommend this famous book to beginners. The game has advanced, but all the basic ideas are there and well expressed.

Reading this book provided just the sort of distraction I needed. When the director called I was completely ready to throw myself into my part.

Already I could see, at odd moments, the fascination of the game. I felt like someone travelling for many hours through a long tunnel, then suddenly catching a glimpse of light and beautiful countryside, followed again by a period of darkness. I half-realized at this time an essential truth about bridge: that it is a very complex game, but in the complexity lies its beauty.

It struck me, too, that, when perfectly played, bridge has the same sort of effect on the heart and mind as any beloved object; to put it another way, that bridge provides as much pleasure as any enterprise in life.

Already I can hear the amateur analysts declaring in learned tones: 'This playboy, the eternal bachelor whom the most beautiful girls in the world cannot resist, who has received many thousands of marriage proposals, who finds beneath his door each night the wildest sexual invitations, who smiles on fortune and on whom fortune smiles, who lives a life of champagne and caviar amid the delights of the Orient and the wildness of Hollywood, this man who has everything disdains easy success; for the first time he has met a problem he cannot master and has been carried away against his will by a new craze.'

This is what people might say about me—and indeed they have said it several times, with every sign of satisfaction.

It is an easy analysis, and like all such it is far from the truth. This book is not written to describe a passion, because no form of indiscretion is more quickly punished than that of telling a friend about a love affair. I write so that others may share my enthusiasm and so that I can live again the brilliant bids and plays I have encountered. Before I begin, I must say that I have never tried to understand or analyse myself. On the contrary, I like to be surprised by my own reactions, both in small affairs and great ones.

I live in the present, the immediate present, a moment that lasts not a day or an hour, but for a minute at most. Self-analysis is for the past or the future, not for the present. When it's hot, I am hot, when it's cool that's good, when I'm hungry I'm hungry when I'm not hungry I'm not hungry. I suppose I sound like an oriental pasha, reclining on cushions and listening to a story told by a delectable houri. The story fades, the pasha yawns, 'I'm bored. . . . Guards! Cut off this one's head. Bring me another.'

I can't help it: that's how I am. I live for the moment; I have no thought for the past or the future; I don't know what will or will not interest me five seconds from now.

Which makes me impossible to live with. . . . It's true, and it's madness for me to live with a woman. Not that I would call for the guard, imaginary or otherwise, when her conversation bored me; on the contrary, every word that passes the lips of a woman moves me profoundly—after all, I must be faithful to my image! Don't forget that I followed Charles Boyer in the role of the archduke who died for love at Mayerling. But forget this image, for this is the truth: it is madness for me to live with a woman, because she finds it maddening to live with me.

Picture me in the most beautiful salon, with gorgeous Louis XVI furnishing, with my closest friends or perhaps with a girl in whom I am extremely interested—in short, a situation in which everything combines to make me happy. We cheerfully discuss the most serious affairs, in truth the most trivial. Then suddenly a clap of thunder, a complete change of mood; for no reason I shall ever understand, I have an overwhelming desire to be alone. It's true; that's what happens.

These changes of mood take me by surprise, but I respond to them immediately, just as a slave obeys the contradictory orders of a tyrannical master. I have to be alone and I say: 'Excuse me, but if you don't mind I'd rather . . .' Rather what? I hardly know myself. Rather not stay in this room and talk to the people there, however charming they may be.

One moment I am lively and amorous, the next I have an overwhelming desire to be alone. I make my excuses and go to my room. I lie on my bed with a book or perhaps run a hot bath and lie with my eyes closed, thinking of nothing. When the mood passes, it passes.

These sudden changes are frequent and ought not to be too much of a problem once they are understood. It should be enough to give your partner fair warning. 'Not to worry,' she will say brightly, 'I quite understand.' Ah, but will she? Put yourself in her place. Her ardent suitor is suddenly transformed into a hermit crossing a desert, an ascetic who yearns for silence and solitude, or one of those fanatics who are only happy when they are on the top of a hill and close to heaven. It is something the most beautiful and generous girl in the world could scarcely tolerate. I understand this very well.

I just have to accept that this is my nature. One thing I have noted is that this strange quirk does not manifest itself when I am engaged in something that interests me. It may be the cinema, bridge, racing—or, of course, a girl (for I mustn't tarnish my public image).

Yes, I am crazy about bridge. The sight, the touch, even the thought of the game excites me. And it all happened because one day I was bored and picked up Goren's book. Like all beginners, I found the game difficult and I determined to master it. Now I want to share my enthusiasm with all my friends, both known and unknown.

During the final sequences of my first film I was so fascinated by my book that when summoned to the set I very nearly brought my career to a sudden end by saying: 'You'll have to wait, I haven't finished the chapter!'

II

One of the strange things about any form of passion is the remarkable change that can occur in a man's head. At first, I didn't appreciate the difference between a passion for bridge and a passion for games of chance. For as far back as I could remember, I had the image of a beautiful young woman with auburn hair who played her personality as well as playing the cards. If I wanted to exaggerate, as most people do when they write their autobiography, I would say that I never saw my mother—for, of course, I am speaking of her—without cards in her hand. Our first house in Alexandria, where I was born, and the splendid mansions we had later in Cairo (my father made a great fortune in business, mostly hardwood) seem in retrospect to have been a succession of sumptuous casinos. The last one, in the most select area of the Garden City, overlooked the Nile between the British and American embassies.

One of the apartments was decorated by my mother in the style of the playing room of a great casino. Today I have business connections with the casino at Trouville and I feel very much in my element when I look round at the lovely gowns and jewels and hear, above the murmur of the players, the click-clack of the little silver ball. I like especially the late hours, when only the real gamblers are left. For them only the game, nothing else, matters. They play till dawn and cannot bear to leave. When the croupier calls 'Last three coups, *messieurs et mesdames,*' they are ready to risk every plaque they have left. This is the moment when they lose the most.

But my mother preferred card games. She played with various friends, and most of all with the portly monarch, King Farouk. These two had the reputation of being the two biggest gamblers in Egypt. And only the Lord knows how many big gamblers there were in Egypt in those days!

King Farouk preferred to play with men; my mother was the exception. At games such as baccarat she was his mascot. He liked her to sit on his left when he dealt the cards and he would begin only when she had cut the pack.

It was supposed to be a favour to sit beside him, but sometimes it was a cruel favour. When they were playing against one another, the stake on a single deal could be anything up to $50,000. But he was always the king, and the game was never a fair one. Sometimes he would claim the pot without even showing his cards, and no one dared to protest when he swept up the money. Such is the royal prerogative!

I remember one game that lasted for several weeks and ended with my mother flat on her back, having lost every necklace, ring, brooch and any other bauble she could lay her hand on. An enthusiastic gambler to this day, my mother sees my passion for cards as an extension of the love we feel for one another. She recalls a game of poker when Farouk, sitting opposite, complained that she was staring at the dark glasses he always wore.

'Ah! Ah!' he growled, genuinely angry. 'You are another one who wants to know whether I am hiding a glass eye.'

There was indeed a rumour that as a result of an accident he had lost an eye and sought to conceal it by wearing the dark glasses that made him such an easy victim for the caricaturists. My mother just smiled in the tactful way that made her such a great hostess.

'Very well,' said the king with a loud laugh in which all the hangers-on joined, 'I'll take off my glasses and you can cry from the rooftops of the town that I haven't got a glass eye.'

And thereafter my mother did indeed cry from the rooftops that the king's eyes were blue-green, intact and very fine.

I wasn't present at this little scene because by this time I was leading the life of all young gentlemen in Cairo. After junior school with the French monks who did so much to spread the French language and culture in the Middle East, I became a pupil at Victoria College, which possessed, among other things, five football grounds for its young students.

As I grew up I discovered the joys of this game. I played mostly with my head, by which I mean my brains, rather than my physique, which was never ideal for sport. I played at right back, and on my good days I was able to foresee where the ball was going and I was generally there. I knew the names of famous players all over the world and the results of important matches; in short, I was a real fan.

Determined to excel—for I had none of the modesty that was instilled into us at Victoria College—I reached international level in 1951 and 1952. I played for Egypt against Brazil and against the great Hungarian team of that era. Alas, I cannot give you a list of the goals I scored, because I was a defender. Attackers had to be fast, and I was not; but I was solid and intelligent enough to be in the right place—or thereabouts.

I had another great hobby at this time—billiards; a game of touch, of course, but also a game calling for mathematical calculation. And I was very interested in mathematics, which for me has always been the most restful pursuit in the world. Nothing to learn, everything to sense and divine. At school I was always a lesson ahead of the class, amusing myself with small problems. This was my nature; I had an easy attitude to life, my mind was like a winding stream which seemingly without effort finds its way past every obstacle.

As a child, I hated everything that demanded an effort of memory. History, geography, chemistry—subjects like these weighed me down and were never mastered. I liked French, English, all languages, because they did not have to be learned from books and fixed in the memory—a process that seemed to me like that of a docker who plonks his load on the quayside without even knowing what it contains.

My dislike of intellectual effort was no doubt one of the reasons why I became an actor. I was always keen on the stage and cinema, and it seemed to me that there was nothing much to learn in this profession. In fact, of course, acting is as difficult and demanding a pursuit as any other. As a child, watching the great actors on screen and stage, I did not appreciate the hard work that lay behind their performances.

In addition to mathematics, I have always been fascinated by crosswords and intellectual puzzles of every kind. It seemed to me that bridge, depending on intuition and good reasoning, was very similar to mathematics. Once the elements were mastered, the rules appeared to be simple: you just had to make tricks, the ace was higher than the king, the king than the queen and so on. Nothing difficult, I thought; just a number of small problems that would lead to the greatest number of tricks. So it seemed to me as I studied Goren's book.

Just a year after my exploits as an international footballer, to the great disappointment of my parents and my teachers, who strongly urged me to follow a career in mathematics, I took to the boards, as they say: I became a professional actor.

III

My feeling for this new game of bridge was wholly platonic. I was like a young man still in his teens who gazes from afar at a beautiful girl but makes no effort to approach her. He realizes that the time has not come and he leaves to chance the moment of making her acquaintance.

At this time we were still living in Alexandria and I was making my second film. It was not an international feature. All the films I made for the first three or four years were for the home market and very successful of their kind.

Sometimes in the evenings I would look in at the hotel where the actors and technicians were staying. After greeting my friends, I would make my way to the card room and watch in silence, as befits a novice. I loved the atmosphere, full of cigar smoke, the staccato bids, the weighty trances, the moments of triumph and despair, muted by the conventions of card-playing.

On one occasion an elderly man, stiff with politeness, approached me and said: 'Excuse me, sir, but we are short of a fourth. Do you by any chance play bridge?'

'Oh yes,' I replied, bouncy as a schoolboy who seeks to astonish his friends.

So it was that I found myself playing with three very amiable strangers. The bidding of the first hand seemed to pass off quite well; at any rate, my partner did not wince when I put down my dummy. On the second hand I was a defender. At one point the declarer led the ace of clubs and I ruffed.

'No clubs?' my partner enquired, with a note of surprise in his voice.

'Oh yes,' I answered cheerfully, 'but I'm ruffing to take the trick.'

The table itself seemed to shrink beneath the gaze of the three players. Then as one voice they declared:

'You don't play a trump when you can follow suit.'

They didn't explain why.

Much mortified by this experience, I didn't venture to play with these good people again. I realized I had misunderstood Mr Goren and went back to read his book again from the beginning.

Some weeks later I played my second game of bridge at a club in Cairo called the Oriental. Don't form a mental picture of an eastern den with damask curtains, hawk-nosed gamblers clustered round the green baize, hieroglyphics on the walls, all in the colours of some eastern Delacroix. The only things oriental about the Oriental were the fans and ventilators that relieved the stifling heat of the summer months. I won't try to describe what it was really like because description is not my strong point; I will say only that the atmosphere suited me and that the club was the rendezvous of the best players in Cairo. I was still a poor player, but it gave me pleasure to play against the strongest opponents. It gave them pleasure too; no one can have had a more expensive bridge education!

To any beginner who asked my advice, I would say that the first requirement is patience. It takes almost as long to learn bridge as to become a Tibetan monk. After six months you know nothing; you begin to have doubts about your intelligence. At most games you would know where you were after this period, but at bridge you wonder whether you will ever improve. The game is like a virtuous maiden: you have to stand rebuffs and endure a long courtship, but what joy when at last the great day arrives!

The moment of truth occurs when cards are drawn in the pairs events. The clubs in France have a system whereby teams are drawn by lot; the player who draws the highest card becomes captain of his team and chooses his partner. As a beginner I was always the last choice, then the second, then the first. This way, you know exactly how you are going up in the world.

As a class, bridge players are very conceited. They are like schoolboys who scarcely deign to recognize a junior. They would rather cut off their tongues than discuss a point of theory with a weaker player.

Is there a player in the world who has not at some point in his career seen his partner frown with dismay when they have cut together? 'Just my luck,' thinks the good player. 'Oh well, it won't last for ever. Perhaps I'll cut against him next time.' The novice grits his teeth, determined to impress. One day a first-class player will speak to him after the game, perhaps even ask his opinion about some bid. Then he will know he has arrived.

It took me three years to become an average player. Only average, but reliable. My partners no longer sighed when they cut me; I was fairly sensible, and I tried very hard. I had already acquired certain habits, which haven't changed. Concentrating on my cards, I smoke all the time; my hand gropes for the packet beside me, I take out a cigarette, carry it to my mouth and light up, all with no break in my concentration.

Apart from these gestures, I see nothing. All my friends at the Oriental knew what I was like and one day they had a bet with me that I wouldn't see a naked girl if she passed within two yards of me. Naturally, I took the bet; after all, I had a certain reputation to maintain!

So one day, everyone else having been forewarned, a gorgeous girl with ruby lips and all the attributes of beauty—it is for your pleasure that I conjure up this description, because I never noticed her—crossed the room where I was engaged in a very tense game.

Everyone in the room, including the players, who are used to concealing their emotions, paid not the slightest attention to this radiant vision. Languorously she settled in a chair beside my partner. Two hands later we won the rubber and I raised my eyes for the first time. There was a great shout of laughter: 'Champagne for everyone!'

The man behind this venture was Léon Yallouze. No one could match his crazy ideas, in life or in bridge. He was an excellent player, but subject on occasions to strange misconceptions. Later, in Paris, we became business partners.

His great friend, Jo-Jo Gresh, was another fine player, and the third in this group was Pierre Schemeil. Pierre had spent part of his youth in France and had stayed at one time in the same apartment as Théron and Desrousseaux, who were the spearhead of the younger generation. In Egypt at this time we discussed many of their ideas.

I Become a Player

IV

My first contact with international players occurred while I was making *Lawrence of Arabia*. (Cinema buffs may recall the famous scene when, from a distance, I came galloping into view on the back of a camel.) There was a break of three months during the filming and the producer thought it would be unsafe for me to return to Egypt. These were troubled times and I might not have been able to obtain an exit visa when I wanted it. The result was that I spent three months in London.

I played mostly at the former Hamilton Club. Boris Schapiro, Rixi Markus, Kenneth Konstam and the redoubtable Dutchman, Bobby Slavenburg, were regular players there. Playing a careful game, I did well at rubber bridge. The secret is simple: if you have good cards, you play them for all they are worth; if you have bad cards, you lose the minimum.

Later in the year I was invited to play in the Egyptian team at the European Championship in Torquay. This, for me, was a most wonderful experience. It was as though a virtuous and beloved maiden had at last dropped all her defences. Imagine! I encountered the best players in Europe, I watched them play, I listened to their discussions, I even joined in.

My principal 'trump'—I knew it well—was not a spade, heart, diamond or club, but the swarthy countenance of Ali, Lawrence's friend. All doors are open for a film actor. Had I been just an unknown member of the Egyptian team, unlikely to finish in the top half of the championship, it would have been a case rather of

'Hi, you, find yourself a broom and sweep the floor. . . .'

Soon after this thrilling experience I had to give up bridge for a while. *Lawrence of Arabia* was shown in America towards the end of 1962. I was nominated for an Oscar for the best supporting role. I had to rush off to Hollywood and devote myself to my career. I received the Oscar and took part in a wild tour to make myself known to American film audiences. It was quite amusing in its way, calling for many of the same qualities that are needed in bridge—qualities such as imagination, steadiness, good sense.

The game was still very much in my thoughts, and a remark of Stendhal occurred to me. Imagine a branch of a tree buried in a salt mine; when it is taken out several months later it will be covered with crystals, sparkling like diamonds. So it was that my passion for bridge continued to glow.

I was very happy to find myself back in Paris at the end of 1963. It was for a film with Gregory Peck and Anthony Quinn, directed by Fred Zinneman, called *Behold a Pale Horse*. In French the title, rather oddly, was *Came the Day of Vengeance*. Those who arrange these matters seem to have a special licence!

As soon as I had found an apartment I hastened to the Avenue Montaigne where, I had been told, I would find the Club de l'Élysée. A small garden, entrance on the ground floor, velvet walls the colour of old gold, crystal chandeliers, grey Louis XVI armchairs, the general effect of a felt-covered jewel box: such was the setting where these clever people, the bridge players of France, disported themselves.

I wandered round the rooms like a cat nonchalantly scenting its new territory. I breathed in the atmosphere. Suddenly I heard familiar voices raised in argument. Impossible! But yes, it was my old friends from the Oriental—Schemeil, Yallouze and Gresh. Belonging to minorities (Yallouze was Jewish, the others Christian), they had decided to leave Egypt and settle in France, which they all knew well. So now we were a foursome and ready for battle!

We played for money and we played high. The top players fought for the privilege of playing matches against us. When we came to the table they welcomed us like gourmets watching the arrival of a tasty selection of cakes. Their smiles faded when they found that the Wild Men (as we were called) were much more formidable than they had supposed. Like the savage who, pursuing a deer in the forest, has no time for refined consideration, we rushed headlong towards the famous 'three notrumps'. All we needed then was to wrap it up. Our bidding was poor, but we knew how to play, and the speed and suddenness of our attack discomfited our opponents.

A typical auction would go: one club—3NT, meaning 'I've a useful hand, we are going to finish in 3NT, so let's get there at once.'

In Egypt, where most of the players were weak, we always made such contracts. In France the outcome was less certain. Our opponents knew how to play the defence and had excellent signalling systems. Even so, we often landed our 3NT contracts and ended with a better score than opponents who had laboriously discovered their 4–4 fit in a major—a proceeding we disdained.

I had few opportunities at this time to put an edge on my game. My film career took up all my time. The 'Rudolf Valentino of the Space Age', as the English journalist, Donald Zec, called me, cast amorous glances from his melting eyes, which (Zec again) made one think of hot chocolate in a sea of vanilla cream. Work, work, work!

During this period I made *The Fall of the Roman Empire* with Sophia Loren, *The Yellow Rolls-Royce* with Ingrid Bergman, *The Fabulous Adventures of Marco Polo*, *Gengis Khan* and many others. I did not have much time to spare for international bridge. To play at the highest level, as in any sport, it is essential to be in regular practice and to play with a partner with whom you have a perfect understanding.

However, I did play in the 1964 Olympiad in New York. Twenty-nine nations competed, from countries as far apart as Kenya and the Dutch Antilles. In the qualifying rounds every team played a match of twenty boards against every other team. I had a great surprise when we sat down to play against Venezuela: the blonde lady on my right was the one who had made my heart beat on the sands of Alexandria, my first true love. Our greatest happiness at that time was to walk hand in hand along the beach or to dance together in the evenings. Neither of us in those days knew anything about the game of bridge. She was French, from Brittany, but she was Protestant. My father, a devoted Catholic, disapproved of our friendship and our ways parted. She married in Alexandria, went to live in Venezuela, and we found one another eleven years later. What happened in the match? Who knows, we were both full of other thoughts.

When we played the United States in this tournament we made an excellent start, gaining on several small boards. Then we lost the whole of our advantage on one deal, all as a result of an unlucky opening lead. This was the hand:

	♠ x x x ♡ A K Q x x x ♢ x x ♣ K x	
♠ Q x ♡ x x x ♢ 10 x x ♣ J 10 8 x x		♠ A K 10 x ♡ J 10 x x ♢ x x ♣ x x x
	♠ J x x x ♡ — ♢ A K Q J x x ♣ A Q x	

In the closed room Awad and his wife played against the formidable Americans, Hamman and Krauss. At one point in the auction Hamman, who was North, bid 4NT. His partner put down his cards, said, 'Excuse me, I must get some fresh air,' and went to the window. After a long interval of deep breathing he returned to the table and bid six diamonds. Awad said to himself, 'What's all this about? I think he has just one ace and solid diamonds.' He led a club and the declarer then had twelve tricks on top.

In the open room I was North and the bidding went like this:

South	*West*	*North*	*East*
Zananiri		Sharif	
—	—	1 ♡	No
2 ♢	No	2 ♡	No
3 ♣	No	4 ♡(1)	dble
5 ♢(2)	No	No	dble
No	No	No	

(1) A mistake; I should have bid simply three hearts and we would then have played in 3NT, the best contract.

(2) He should have passed, I think, but four hearts also goes down.

West led the queen of spades and the defence made the first four tricks for a penalty of 500.

I remember my bad hands much more than my good ones. So please don't talk about my vanity!

During this event I came to know the members of the famous Italian Blue Team. (At Torquay Italy had fielded a sort of second eleven.) I admired them all and especially Benito Garozzo, who is a positive magician at the game, excelling equally in theory and practice. Also, he has the most extraordinary effect on his opponents. I remember very well an occasion at Deauville—and don't say I am making it up, because many people were watching on bridgerama at the time. Benito, who had bid diamonds and spades, was playing in four spades. The defenders, two very well-known players from Portugal, had already made three tricks and the player sitting East still had the king of diamonds over dummy's A x. For some extraordinary reason he led the king of diamonds and gave away the contract. 'Sorry, partner, I pulled the wrong card.' Yes, well, people do 'pull the wrong card' when they play against Benito.

I greatly enjoyed making films in Italy, because I had a very special relationship with the bridge players. The game is so colourful there, full of surprises, with a childlike quality one does not find in France. And they're so superstitious, even the hardened tournament players!

In Turin there is a young lady who is famous for the bad luck she brings. Her reputation follows her wherever she goes. It is said that when she boards a ship it sinks before weighing anchor; if she enters a lift it is likely to stop for no reason between two floors. This Jonah appeared one evening at a hotel where I was playing in a championship.

'Omar, Omar,' whispered a friend, 'whatever you do, don't let that woman near your table.'

'Don't be silly,' I replied. 'I'm by way of being a mathematician. I'm certainly not superstitious.'

So I sat down to play and, as you have guessed, this woman took a chair beside my table. I paid not the slightest attention to her. Then came a hand which I played in seven diamonds with A K Q 10 opposite four small. And, of course, the player on my left held J x x x.

I left the table for a moment and spoke to Léon Yallouze. 'Léon,' I said, 'I need your help. Will you book a suite in the hotel and make all the arrangements?'

Then I went back and said to the lady: '*Mademoiselle*, would you be so kind as to go with my friend, order champagne, caviar, whatever you fancy, and remain in the room till the end of the session?'

I don't know whether she took this to be a romantic suggestion. All I do know is that next morning Léon said to me: 'Well, what happened? Was there a flood? A fire?'

V

I had to work very hard at this time. The fact is that I was the only actor in the West who could say to a woman 'I love you' without causing an outburst of laughter in the front stalls. Since it was a period when there was a great demand for love stories, I was sent rushing from one end of the world to the other in pursuit of romance. It never stopped.

If I entered a restaurant at this time and was recognized by the orchestra leader, he immediately struck up the theme song of *Doctor Zhivago*. Women expected always to see me enveloped in a great mantle of fur. I had to abandon this image to trim my hair and alter the colour of my eyebrows for the role of the general in Anatole Litvak's film *The Night of the Generals*. I can say with some confidence that I looked a good deal more German than Peter O'Toole, Tom Courtenay or Joanna Pettit!

After my affray with Hitler, I became Sophia Loren's lover in *La Belle et le Cavalier*. The film was made in the little town of St Vincent (a self-governing enclave in the north of Italy). Here I fulfilled the dream of all players—not card players, but gamblers.

On the last night there was a gala, and I found myself in intimate conversation with a young starlet, full of promise. But alas! The promises were concerned more with her career than with myself. She declined the invitation to partake of a last drink in my room. Thwarted again (as they used to say in the melodramas), I had a last drink on my own in the bar of the casino. Then I put every chip I had left on 29. It came up. I left it there and it came up again. I switched to 14, and it was the same again. Suddenly the croupiers laid a black cloth over the table. I had broken the bank. I had won 190 million old francs. They brought me a basket to carry away my chips. I was surrounded by a pack of hounds, and what with one thing and another I was down to 170 million when I woke the next morning. Even so. . . .

The following winter I was at St Moritz and played bridge with the Shah of Iran. Receiving my invitation from a prince in his suite, I put on my 'smoking', as we call it, and made my way to a beautiful villa. The dinner, at which the Belgian Ambassador was also present, was excellent; everything I like best, especially rice and caviar. I wondered whether it would be lawful, or prudent, to double the Emperor of Persia, the King of Kings.

As it turned out, I was assigned to partner the Shah, so it was left to the Belgian Ambassador to decide this tricky point. He played with the Queen, Farah Diba, an inexperienced but very intelligent player. The King himself had a somewhat ponderous approach to the game, as I soon discovered.

I opened one spade.

He responded two clubs.

I bid two hearts; he passed; and I went down.

I inquired respectfully why, holding Q x x of spades, he had not given me a preference in this suit. He replied: 'You didn't rebid spades.'

He had some very odd ideas about the game, but what I remember best is the twenty kilos of Iranian rice that he most kindly delivered to my hotel the next day. I thought to myself: What a fool! I should have said how much I admired the Queen's jewels.

VI

I was making a lot of money at this time, but I knew nothing about investments and financial affairs in general. One day Léon Yallouze, who was acting as my business manager, proposed an interesting and challenging idea: to form a professional team to play against the strongest opposition all over the world. There would be a big public for matches of this kind, partly from local pride and partly because of my name.

Kramer had had the same idea for tennis players twenty years before, and it had worked pretty well!

We knew where to find the best players: Italy, where distances were not great and the top players could meet often for practice. Benito Garozzo, Giorgio Belladonna and Pietro Forquet were chartered, plus Claude Delmouly, my regular partner in France. Expenses were paid, but the team did not receive salaries; they all had their professions—Garozzo was a jeweller in Rome, Belladonna a bridge journalist, Forquet a bank director, Delmouly a bridge teacher. As for myself, the matches would be played when I was not professionally engaged.

So the Omar Sharif Bridge Circus was formed. Meanwhile Ira Corn, a millionaire from Texas, had much the same idea in America. He had enormous means at his disposal: a colossal fortune and the choice of several hundred fine players. He appointed a coach, and the members of his team, Bobby Wolff, Jim Jacoby, Billy Eisenberg, Robert Goldman, Bob Hamman and others, worked full time and were provided with big salaries, a psychoanalyst and a masseur. These were the Dallas Aces, the name recalling the Four Aces of pre-war days.

Our team was usually Garozzo and Belladonna, Delmouly and myself. Forquet played when he could spare the time, Yallouze seldom. It was better that way. At the beginning he played once with Garozzo. They were at odds with one another after the first quarter of an hour.

Yallouze had doubled a contract because he was void in the trump suit. Garozzo was quite wild: 'You don't double with a void in trumps!'

'Why not? Don't you want me to protect your queen to four?'

'I didn't have queen to four. I had two small.'

The arguments between these two while we were forming the Circus had me knocking my head against the wall. Damned wreckers! They always criticized when the result of the hand was known. It would go like this: 'You had A K x of clubs opposite x x. You should have begun by playing low from each hand.'

'What?' I would say. 'Why low from each hand?'

'Because that's the right play.'

Our system was the Blue Team Club, and our first three matches were played before most enthusiastic audiences in Holland. For players of every class, it is extremely interesting to follow the play on bridgerama. All the time the spectator is thinking, 'What would I do in this situation?' and then he sees how the experts handle it. (Of course, the audience can see all four hands.) It is less spectacular than tennis or football, but the viewer can identify much better with the performers. If you are watching Borg play tennis you can't really say to yourself, 'I wouldn't have given Connors a chance to smash, I would have aimed a low ball at the white line in the corner.' But when you are watching a bridge game you can always feel you would have done better than the players.

We won our matches in Holland, Italy and London. Our first defeat was in a match against the Benelux countries at The Hague. Undoubtedly this was due to the absence of Garozzo, who was unable to leave his *bijoux* in Rome.

This was the hand that killed us:

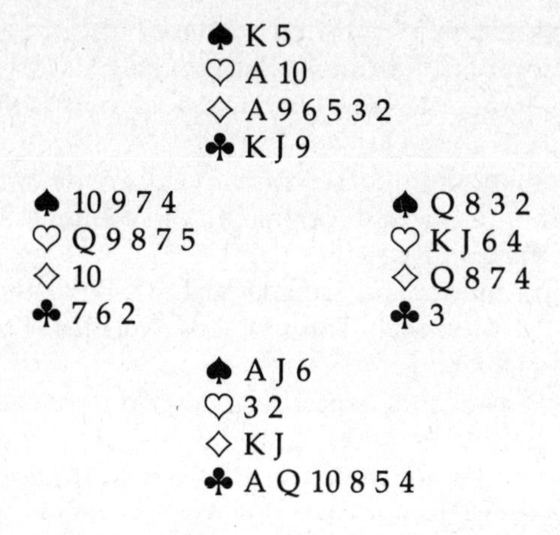

In the Blue Club system an opening bid of two clubs is natural. Belladonna was the dealer and this was our sequence:

South	*North*
Belladonna	Sharif
2 ♣	2 ◇
2NT	3 ◇
3 ♠	4NT
5 ◇	7 ♣
No	

My first response of two diamonds was conventional, asking the opener to describe his hand.

South's 2NT meant that he had six clubs and high honours in two other suits.

Three diamonds was again conventional, asking, 'Which suits?'

The rebid of three spades showed controls in spades and diamonds.

My bid of 4NT asked for more information and the response of five diamonds signified ace or king of the suit.

I bid seven clubs with every confidence, but on this occasion 'God was not Italian'. West led a heart and Giorgio had to win with the ace. The lead cost him an important entry. He cashed two clubs, then led the king and jack of diamonds. West ruffed and we were one down. (It would not have helped, obviously, to draw three rounds of trumps; Belladonna's line would have worked if by chance the same hand had held three clubs and four diamonds.)

At the other table Forquet led a spade against the same contract of seven diamonds. With the extra entry in dummy, Slavenburg easily made the grand slam.

We went to America and Canada next. Yallouze had arranged big matches at Montreal, Toronto, Los Angeles, Dallas, New Orleans and New York.

Are you by any chance expecting a description of my amorous adventures on the way, of the occasions when I played the subtle seducer? No, that's not my style. I have a reputation for being discreet, and though sometimes this weighs on me more heavily even than Dr Zhivago's famous cape, it has many advantages. And I'm not thinking only of being offered enormous sums to play opposite an actress so beautiful that the whole world dreams about her.

Living intensely in the present, and giving little thought to past history, my memories are in no sort of order. I will just describe the places, the partners, the triumphs and disasters as they occur to me.

VII

Bridge historians are advised not to read this chapter—or, indeed, anything that follows. Too bad if, as might happen in *Hellzapoppin*, a charge of Red Indians is accompanied by sentimental music, or if our team is recorded as playing against another team that could not possibly have been in the same place at that time. As the psychoanalysts (a tribe I detest) say, it's feelings that count. I am much too lazy to check all the facts.

However, I am fairly certain that in Toronto we had the pleasure of playing a match against the Canadians I had met at Deauville—notably Sammy Kehela and Eric Murray, who had just won the Spingold Trophy in America.

Garozzo was back in the team: Garozzo, with his air of an aloof fakir and his extraordinary flair.

It was a really tough match. After twenty boards there was nothing in it. Then I was the hero with an inspired opening lead.

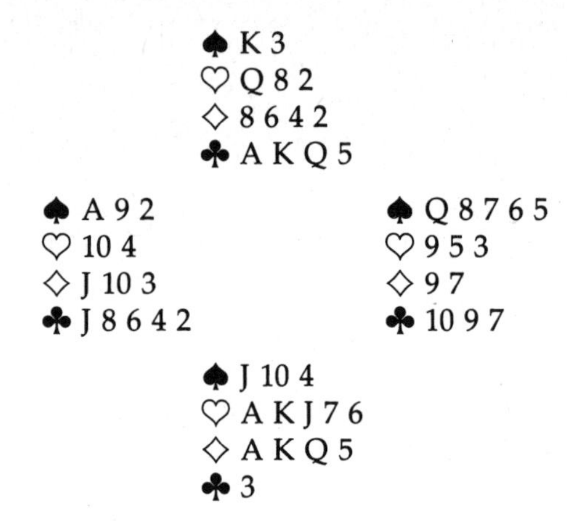

I was West, Belladonna was East, and the contract was six hearts by South. I was on lead. All the spectators had their eyes on me, or rather on the film star, Omar Sharif. And Omar wondered, what would Lawrence's trusty friend, Ali, have done in this situation? It looked from the bidding as though North held the control in spades. I led a small spade from my A x x.

The declarer, quite naturally, played low from dummy. My partner won with the queen and returned a spade. One down, and it was the only way to beat the contract.

The public now saw me in a new light. I was no longer a star of the silver screen; I was a bridge champion, thanks to a small spade. As Robert Hamman remarked, to be a winner at bridge you have to visualize the cards in the unseen hands.

Suddenly I was a bridge star. Another deal from the Toronto match showed the extraordinary skill and judgement of Belladonna and Garozzo:

♠ Q 10 x x
♡ A Q x
◇ A x
♣ J 9 x x

♠ A K J x x
♡ x x x
◇ x
♣ A Q 10 x

North (Belladonna) opened one spade and East made a weak jump overcall of three diamonds. Not so easy now, you may think, to play in clubs rather than in spades. But watch:

South	*West*	*North*	*East*
Garozzo	Elliot	Belladonna	Sheardown
—	—	1 ♠	3 ◇
4 ◇	No	4 ♠	No
5 ◇!	No	5NT!!	No
6 ♣!!	No	No	No

In a system which uses a conventional one club opening it is usually difficult to finish in clubs unless great length is held. But here, as you see, the Italians finished in clubs despite holding nine spades!

North's four spades said, 'I have no other suit I can show at a safe level.' When South persisted with another cue bid, Belladonna said, in effect, 'Well, if you are not interested in spades, I do hold another four-card suit.' And this suit had to be clubs, because he could have shown hearts by bidding five hearts over five diamonds.

As good players well know, there is often an advantage in playing with a trump suit divided 4–4 in preference to another suit divided 5–4. This hand is an example: in spades the declarer must find both kings right; in clubs it is sufficient to find just one king on the right side because a heart from North can be discarded on the fifth spade.

I shall never forget our match at Los Angeles. I went down in a contract I would have made if I had taken a special precaution. Look first at the North–South cards:

♠ K 8 7 4
♡ K 9 3
♢ A K Q 2
♣ J 5

♠ A 9
♡ J 10 8 5 2
♢ J 10
♣ Q 10 6 3

I played in four hearts after West had opened one club. West began with ace, king and another club. East played the 2, 8, 9, and I won the third round with the queen.

What now? To lead the jack of hearts would be a mistake because it would allow West to go up with the ace and play a fourth club. I would have to ruff in dummy and would be in great danger of losing another trick in the trump suit.

You saw that? So did I! I played three rounds of diamonds, safely discarding my fourth club, then came to hand with the ace of spades and led the jack of hearts. West won with the ace and played a second spade. I was in dummy now and had to decide whether to return to hand (for a heart finesse) with a spade ruff or a diamond ruff. I chose the spade—fatal, for the full hand was:

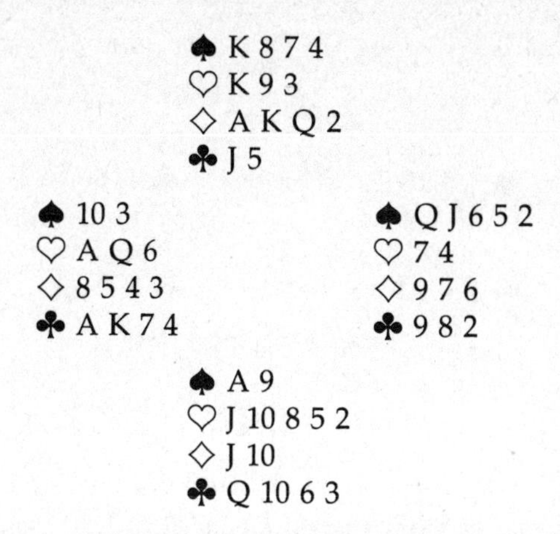

You see how the play went: three rounds of clubs, three diamonds, spade to ace, heart to ace, spade from West, then a third spade, overruffed.

What was my mistake? Are you sure you've seen it? The third spade, instead of a diamond, was unlucky—a 'wrong view', as bridge players call it. The *mistake* was in failing to play king of spades, then a spade to the ace. Had I done this, I would not have found myself in dummy at an embarrassing moment.*

Dallas, for most people, is cowboy country; for bridge players it is Aces country, where the professional players train all day with their coach. At least, that's what we were given to understand . . .

We landed to a fabulous reception, perhaps more in honour of a film star than a team of bridge players. The orchestra played the Omar Sharif refrain, the one from *Doctor Zhivago*. I was surrounded by a crowd of young autograph hunters, while the pretty majorettes whirled their batons as they marched up and down the aerodrome.

We narrowly beat the Aces in a match of seventy-two boards. I remember particularly this one:

*In one of my brighter efforts of nomenclature I once called this form of play the 'dentist's coup', because of the element of extraction. T.R.

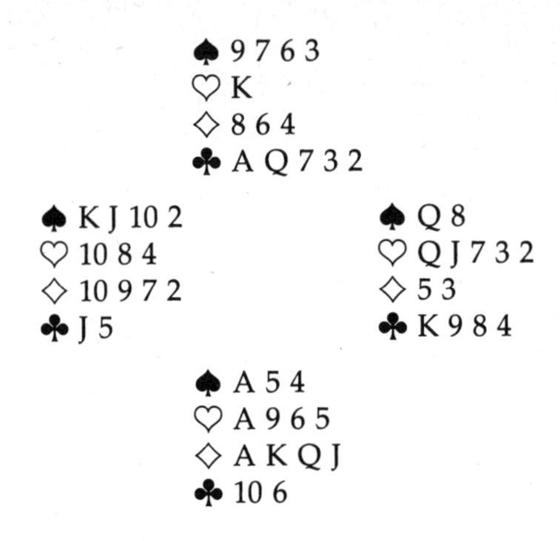

I was in 3NT and West led the jack of clubs. It is tempting to play the queen, but fortunately I saw in time that this would be a mistake, as it would allow East to win and return a heart. To make sure of my ninth trick I went up with the ace of clubs and followed with a low club to the 10.

An extraordinary incident took place that night. Bridge players need not read the rest of this chapter, which will be of interest only to the madly erotic.

About four or five in the morning, exhausted after the game, I returned to my room in the very sumptuous motel that one finds in Dallas. All I wanted was to get out of my smoke-filled evening dress, take a bath and find the strength to meet, in a few hours' time, the journalists who would want to know whether I was happiest in the role of Sheik Ali, Doctor Zhivago or Prince Rudolph.

I was looking in the mirror to check whether I would ever look right for next morning's photo session, when there was a knock on the door. I opened it and found myself face to face with a woman in a green dress, thirty to thirty-five, dead drunk. She gave me a hefty push and entered the room. Hardly looking at me, she announced: 'You are going to make love to me.'

'Madam, please, it is very late and. . . .'

In a polite but firm manner I took her by the elbow and propelled her towards the door. She broke away, opened her bag, and produced a small revolver, very feminine, with a mother-of-pearl grip. In a much less feminine tone she said: 'Take off your clothes.'

It was a moment impossible to imagine unless you have experienced it. And I wouldn't wish it on anybody. To look at the muzzle of a revolver, such a pretty little revolver, but in the hands of someone far from sane. . . . I said to her: 'Madam, be reasonable, I. . . .'

I don't know what Rudolph Valentino or Charles Boyer would have done in this situation. All I could do was stammer: 'Madam, please. . . .'

'Take off your clothes.'

They would both have done the same as I did: they would have begun to undress.

She undressed too, awkwardly, keeping the revolver pointed at me. She lay on the bed and commanded: 'Come and make love to me.'

I stood in front of her, my knees shaking.

'Madam, you can see, it's quite impossible.'

She could see.

'Come closer.'

I took two paces towards her. Using her free hand, she sought to encourage me. In vain. As it would have been with anyone from Errol Flynn to Johnny Weismuller. After a few moments she hissed at me: 'You are a fraud!'

No doubt that is how Omar Sharif appeared to her in her drunken state. She dressed quickly, using both hands now.

'You are a fag,' was her parting shot, as she replaced the revolver in her bag and left as quickly as she had come.

American women are the most shameless I have ever known. A few days after this experience I came back to my room late at night after playing a match, and as I was trying to relax I caught sight of a couple of feet peeping out from under my bed. It is quite alarming to think you are alone in your room and see a couple of feet under your bed.

On this occasion it was a teenager who had somehow slipped into my room and had been waiting for several hours. Fortunately, this one was not carrying a revolver, and after providing her with my autograph I was able to lead her gently to the door.

VIII

It is time to return to the bridge table.

One day in New Orleans, just before our match was due to begin, I caught sight of Garozzo dancing along the street to a jazz rhythm, looking like an Italian bear that had found its pot of honey. In the match that followed we were 30 points down at the first interval but recovered to win by 94.

Benito is the gentlest, most civilized man in the world until he has thirteen cards in his hand. Then he becomes a demon, seeking every possible way to cause alarm and despondency.

In the second half of the match there was an example of his skill in recovering from what might have been a catastrophic decision.

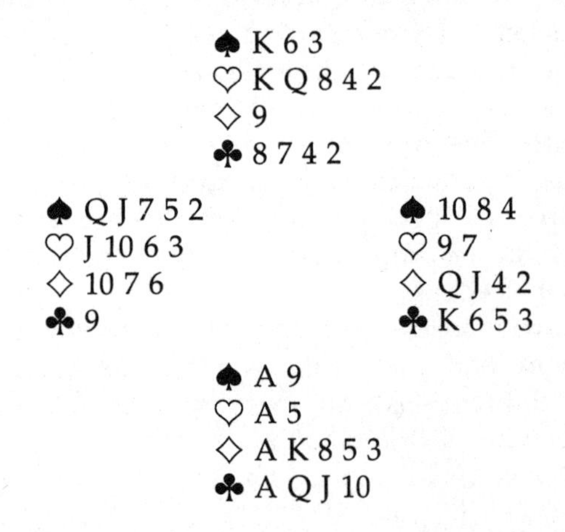

Benito opened as South with a conventional one club, and West made a (very) weak jump overcall of two spades. Belladonna doubled; this promised at least 6 points with not more than two controls.

The partnership finished in six clubs and West led the queen of spades. Benito won with the ace, took a diamond ruff and finessed the queen of clubs, which held.

It is possible now, as the cards lie, to make all thirteen tricks (diamond ruff, club finesse, king of diamonds, then play winners from dummy). However, Benito quite naturally thought West was holding up the king of clubs and so laid down the ace. Disaster! West showed out and East still held K x. Undeterred, Benito played ace and king of hearts, arriving at this position:

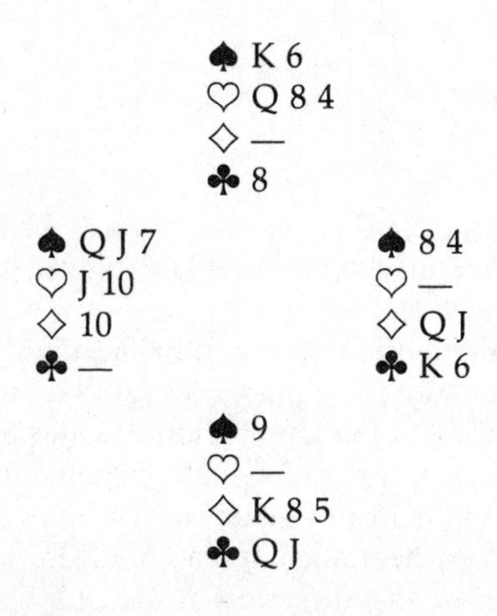

The queen of hearts was led from dummy and East decided to throw a diamond. South did the same, then followed with king of spades and a spade ruff. A diamond was ruffed in dummy, and at this point a heart from the table ensured the twelfth trick.

It looks as though East would have done better to ruff the queen of hearts with the king of clubs. There are then two possible defences. If East exits with his last club, South cashes the king of diamonds and leads his second club, squeezing both opponents; and if East, after ruffing with the club king, exits with a spade to the king, South ruffs a spade, plays king and another diamond, and still has a master trump.

The final match of our tour was in New York, one of my

favourite cities. The Italians loved it too. You should have seen them every evening, consuming mountains of spaghetti! This was a famous hand:

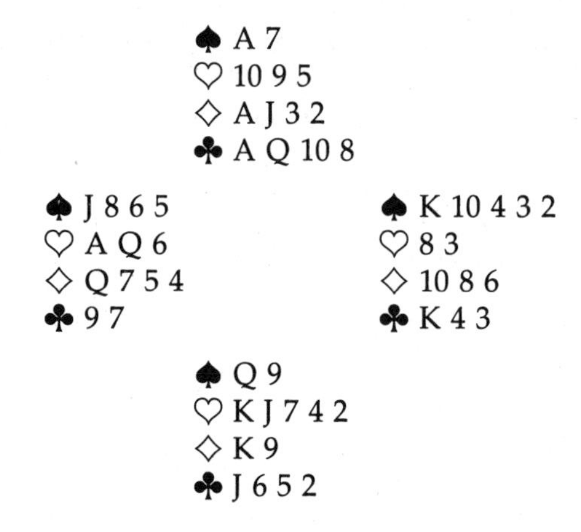

Howard Schenken played the South hand in four hearts and Belladonna led the 9 of clubs. Schenken played the 10 from dummy. And Garozzo ducked!

The 10 of hearts ran to the queen and Belladonna led a second club. Schenken, normally a fast player, thought for a long while. Had Belladonna underled the king? Should South finesse again or should he go up with the ace? Finally, Schenken played low from dummy, the king won and a club was returned. One down!

I also played in four hearts against a club lead. I played low from dummy, but now the king won and a club was returned. When West won the first round of hearts with the queen, he switched to a low spade. I went up with the ace and took the diamond finesse to dispose of my second spade. So I lost just one club and two trumps.

At dinner that evening I complimented Benito on his defence.

'Not good,' he replied, winding the next big mouthful of spaghetti round his fork. 'Like Stayman at the other table, I should win with the king of clubs and return a club. The declarer runs the 10 of hearts. Giorgio wins with the *ace* and leads a spade. South goes up with the ace and runs ♡9. Giorgio wins, puts me in with the king of spades, and I give him a club ruff. Two down.' He laughed shortly and resumed his attack on the spaghetti.

IX

In 1970 the British players Jeremy Flint and Jonathan Cansino issued a novel type of challenge: a match of eighty rubbers at very high stakes indeed—£1 a point (£100 a hundred) and a substantial side-stake on each group of four rubbers.

We played in front of big audiences in the ballroom of the Piccadilly Hotel, with frequent attention from radio and television. It was a national event and excellent publicity for the game. Ladbroke, the big bookmakers, took a great deal of money on the home team, who ended up at odds on with our team at evens.

One of the conditions was that I should play at least sixty rubbers. I played partly with Delmouly and partly with Garozzo. The decisive rubbers, undoubtedly, were played by Garozzo and Belladonna.

We started badly, not making the most of some good cards. Two examples follow of what the French call 'spilt cream'—that is to say, badly missed opportunities.

♠ A K J 9 7
♡ K J 9 5
◇ Q 9 4
♣ 6

♠ 5
♡ A Q 8 7 4
◇ A K 7
♣ A Q 8 3

This was the bidding by Delmouly and myself:

South	*North*
Sharif	Delmouly
1 ♣	1NT
2 ♡	3 ♡
4 ♣	4 ♠
4NT	5 ♣
5 ◇	5 ♠
6 ♡	No

One club was conventional, and the response of 1NT promised four controls (two for an ace, one for a king).

Two hearts was natural, and the raise to three hearts confirmed the suit.

After the cue-bids in clubs and spades my 4NT was what we call a 'general try', asking for further information.

I failed to bid the grand slam because I thought my partner might hold ace-king of spades and king of clubs. Over five spades I should have bid 5NT, and with his good trumps Delmouly would surely have bid seven hearts.

With Benito, a few hands later, it was the opposite story.

♠ K 8 3
♡ A 8 7
♢ A Q J 10 6 4
♣ 10

♠ Q 5 4
♡ K
♢ K 8 5 2
♣ K Q 9 7 6

Belladonna, South, opened one diamond and the bidding continued:

South	*North*
Belladonna	Garozzo
1 ♢	1 ♡
2 ♣	4 ♢
4 ♡	4 ♠
4NT	5 ♣
5 ♢	6 ♢
No	

North's four diamonds set the suit and Belladonna showed his cheapest control, as the system demands. His 4NT on the next round was meant to say 'I have nothing else to show', but perhaps Garozzo misread it. So they finished in a slam with two aces missing.

I am usually the cautious one, but I had to take the blame for another misadventure during this first day.

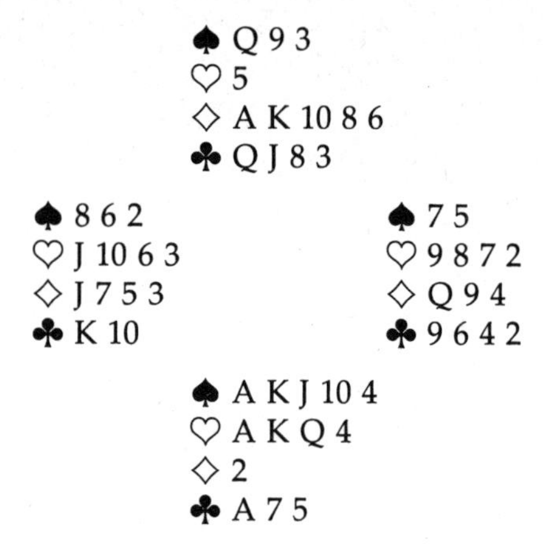

Benito opened one diamond as North and I responded one heart, following the *canapé* style in which the shorter suit is bid first on good hands. The bidding continued:

South	*North*
Sharif	Garozzo
—	1 ◇
1 ♡	1NT
2 ♠	3 ♠
4 ♣	4 ◇
4 ♡	4 ♠
4NT	5 ◇
5 ♡	6 ♠
7 ♠	No

As before, after suit agreement we exchanged cue-bids. I should perhaps have taken more note of the fact that Benito's five diamonds over my 4NT denied control in clubs. Still, I think that most players would have taken a chance on the grand slam. In the end I had to take the club finesse. It was an annoying hand because there are enough entries to establish a long diamond, but you cannot ruff a heart as well.

We recovered the lost points by the end of the day. Note one clever play by Belladonna:

♡ 8

♡ K 10 5 ♡ Q 9 7 6 4 3 2

♡ A J

South played in 3NT after East had made a weak jump overcall in hearts. 'West will lead a low heart and the suit will be blocked,' the commentator predicted. But Giorgio, departing from convention, led the *king* of hearts and the contract was defeated.

On a later deal Benito made a very clever play and I am sorry to say that I did not fully co-operate.

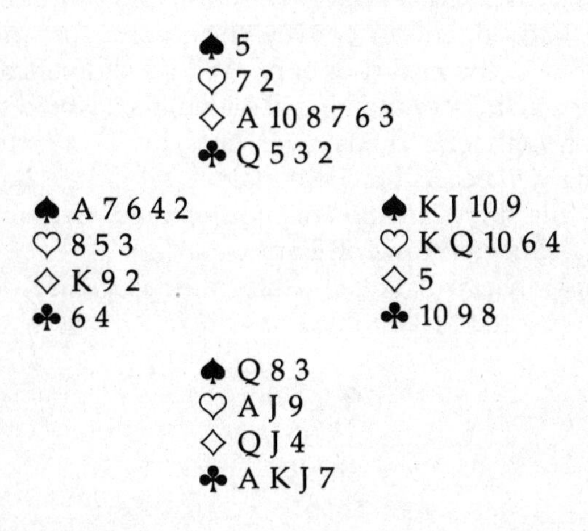

The bidding went:

South	*West*	*North*	*East*
Cansino	Sharif	Flint	Garozzo
1 ♣	No	1 ◇	No
2NT	No	3 ♣	No
3NT	No	No	No

Cansino played extremely well in this match, but his 3NT was surely a mistake. If he bids three diamonds the partners will finish in five of a minor, which depends simply on the diamond finesse.

Realizing that South had the hearts well held, I began with a low spade. Unfortunately for us, the suit was blocked. On lead after four rounds of spades, Garozzo made the shrewd play of a *low* heart; it was certain that the declarer would not finesse at this point and Benito wanted to create a false picture of the lie of the heart honours. You will see the importance of this in a moment.

South won with the ace of hearts and played four rounds of clubs. Now I made a mistake: I let go two hearts instead of one heart and one diamond.

The declarer followed with the queen of diamonds, on which I played low. Now a long, long trance; finally Cansino took the finesse and made the contract. By leading a low heart at trick five, Garozzo had sought to convey the impression that he was missing one of the heart honours. And if I had held a top heart, five spades to the ace, and king of diamonds, I would surely have overcalled with one spade over one club. Unfortunately, by discarding two hearts I made it plain that I did *not* hold K x x or Q x x in this suit; Cansino was not tempted, therefore, to play East for a singleton king of diamonds.

The most spectacular deal, which caused a great amount of ink to flow, occurred on the third day.

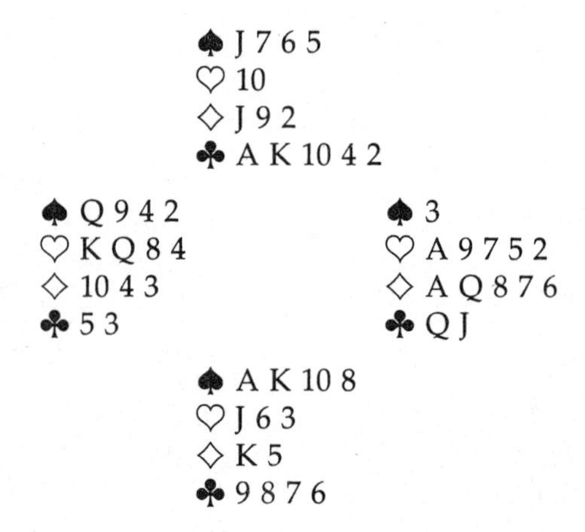

Both sides were vulnerable and this was the bidding:

South	*West*	*North*	*East*
Flint	Delmouly	Cansino	Sharif
—	—	No	1 ♡
No	2 ♡	dble	4 ♡
4 ♠	dble	No	No
No			

Delmouly led the king of hearts and I signalled with the 9. A second heart was ruffed low in dummy and a low spade ran to the 10 and queen. (It would, in fact, have been better play to run the jack, leaving a low spade in dummy and preserving the A K 10.) After long thought Delmouly switched to a diamond. I won and returned a diamond. South now crossed to the ace of clubs, on which I dropped the queen. Trumps were drawn and a veritable fortune now depended on the view in clubs. Flint finessed and did not make another trick; down 1100, instead of plus 790.

Two points arise. When in with the queen of spades Delmouly could have defeated the contract by leading another heart; dummy ruffs, the jack of spades is cashed, and declarer leads a diamond. I go up with the ace, naturally, and play another heart, establishing a second trump trick for the defence. Claude has always maintained that my 9 of hearts, in our system, indicated strength in diamonds; he placed me with A K of diamonds and declarer with the queen of clubs.

The second point concerns Jeremy's finesse of the 10 of clubs. This placed me, in effect, with 6–5–1–1 distribution. Well, it was not impossible; the critics maintained that with this distribution I would have removed the double of four spades, but it's not certain.

Finally, I must mention a particularly fine decision by Delmouly, which astonished all the commentators and critics.

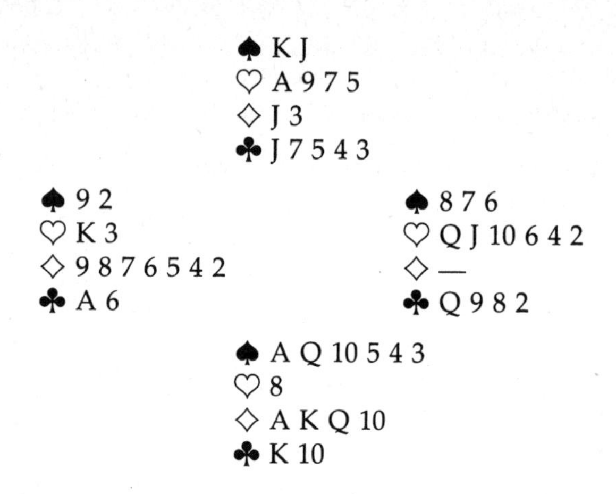

South opened with a conventional one club and the bidding proceeded as follows:

South	*West*	*North*	*East*
Delmouly	Cansino	Sharif	Flint
1 ♣	2 ◇	2NT	No
3 ♠	No	4 ♠	No
No!!	No		

A diamond was led and ruffed, and a low club came back. South had to play low to be sure of making just four spades.

All the critics wondered how Delmouly came to pass four spades. My 2NT had indicated, in the system, three controls—two for the ace of hearts, one for the king of spades. Delmouly judged, quite rightly, that if I had held a control in diamonds (a singleton), I would have shown this over three spades. Thus, from his angle, the fourth diamond might have been a loser. Apart from which, there might have been two club losers.

Our team won in the end by 5740, that is to say £57,400, plus a number of side-bets at £1000 each. The English pair held more kings, queens and jacks than we did, but we held sixteen more aces. Our game bidding was slightly superior, I think, but in our slam bidding we were below form.

As a promotion, the match was a tremendous success. I think I can say, too, that the standard of play was exceptionally high, especially when it is remembered that we played for very long hours (often two or three hours after the public session had ended). And despite the very high stakes, the entire match was played in the best possible spirit.

X

From London we returned to the New World for a fantastic series of matches against the Aces. We played in seven big towns: Chicago, Winnipeg, Los Angeles, St Paul, Dallas, Detroit, and Philadelphia. But while the Aces were able to rest in the afternoons, we had to play forty boards against the local champions in the afternoons and forty against the Aces in the evenings. In addition, I had to play my role as a film star and also give publicity to the playing card manufacturers who bore the expenses of the tour, not to mention the endless signing of autographs; no wonder I found it difficult to maintain my image.

I remember three hands in particular, the first a 'silent coup' by Billy Eisenberg, whom they call the 'Machine Man' because of his consistency and imperturbability.

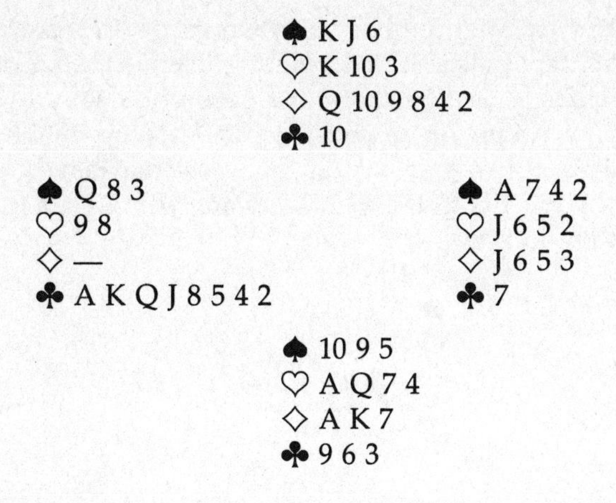

1NT by Garozzo, South. Pass by Billy Eisenberg, West. Three diamonds by Belladonna, saying, 'This is probably the right contract, but if you have good support for diamonds, perhaps. . . .' Pass by East, 3NT by Garozzo, who did indeed have a good fit in diamonds. Pass by Eisenberg, sounding like a man going to his own funeral, and pass by North and East. The defenders took the first nine tricks.

In the match at Dallas Bobby Wolff and I both missed a chance to enter our names in the history books. You hold as West:

♠ 8 7
♡ J 7 2
◇ 10 9 7
♣ K 9 8 6 5

The bidding goes:

South	*West*	*North*	*East*
—	—	—	1 ♡
dble	No	2 ♡	3 ♡
3 ♠	No	4NT	No
5 ♣	No	6 ♠	dble
No	No	No	

After South's take-out double North has carried the partnership to a slam. Since West himself holds a useful-looking card, the king of clubs, it seems likely that East's double is of the Lightner variety, asking for an unusual lead—not the suit he has bid and not a trump. Well, it looks as though he may have a void in clubs. Wolff and I both led a low club after similar auctions. Now look at the full deal:

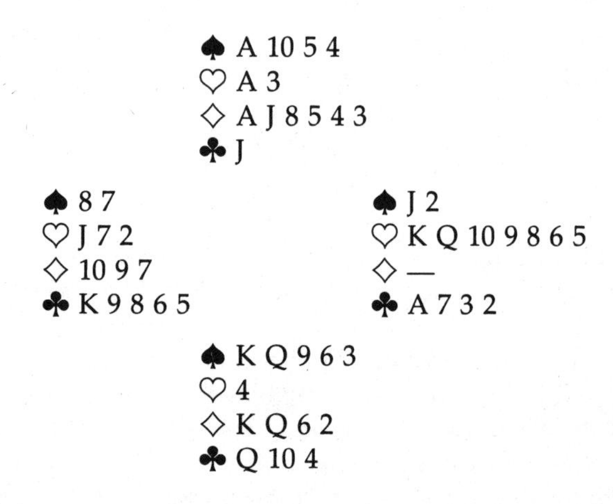

As you see, the contract was lay-down after the club lead. 'Sorry, partner, from my side it looked more likely you would be void of clubs than diamonds.' Ah, but what about leading the *king* of clubs? As the cards lie, East plays low and ruffs a diamond at trick two; and if East holds a void in clubs, he will ruff the king and make his second trick, wherever it lies.

Finally, a great play by Belladonna from the match at Winnipeg:

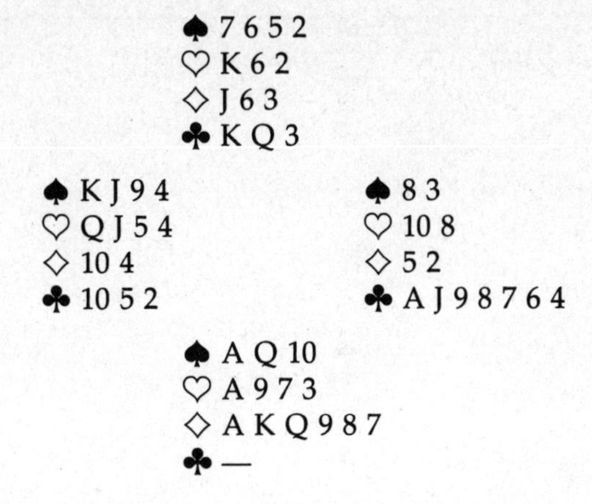

At both tables East opened with a pre-emptive four clubs and South became declarer in six diamonds. Garozzo, in particular, was under strength for this bid, which in the Italian systems is not a simple shut-out. Goldman, quite reasonably, took the spade finesse and lost one spade and one heart.

Belladonna, having noted that American players seemed to favour weak pre-empts, played on the assumption that West would hold the king of spades and also the length in hearts. But there are only ten tricks on top and it is not easy to see how the declarer can develop two more.

After ruffing the club lead and discarding the 10 of spades on the master club, Giorgio played trumps to arrive at this position:

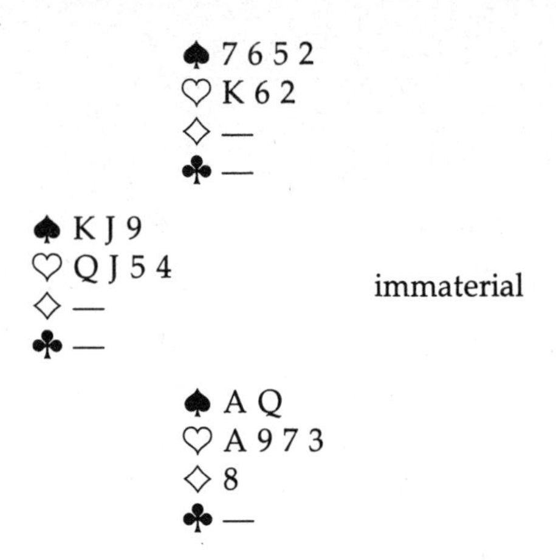

Now South led the last diamond. What can West do? If he throws a spade, South will play ace and another, establishing two spade winners in dummy; if a heart, he will be thrown in on the third round, forced to lead a spade and at the same time concede a trick to the thirteenth heart. A few moments later Eisenberg surrendered and the bridgerama audience broke into thunderous applause.

XI

If the leading American players are driving around in motor cars, they are driving Lancias, thanks to me. Every time they open the doors they must, I imagine, think of me with gratitude. It's as though I had made them a present.

This happened in 1972. On this occasion the Omar Sharif Circus was sponsored by Lancia. All our expenses were paid, and I continued to play with Belladonna and Forquet, which was very enjoyable.

The arrangement was that we would play matches in four towns and if we were beaten each of our six opponents would be presented with a Lancia. The directors thought it would be excellent publicity, win or lose. In any case our team, Belladonna–Garozzo, Forquet–Sharif, looked unbeatable.

But things didn't turn out quite as expected. Our first match was in New York. There was nothing in it when we came to the last board.

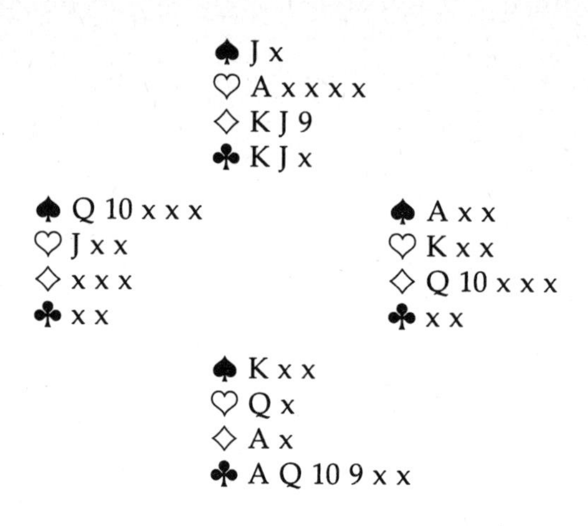

Granovetter, South, played in six clubs. Forquet led a diamond, because I had doubled this suit during the auction. Granovetter, who had not seemed very pleased with the dummy, put in the 9, which was covered by the 10 and ace. After two rounds of trumps a low spade was led from dummy. I thought to myself, it's not likely he has a singleton king, but if I let him win this trick I may be in difficulties later. So I went up with the ace of spades and returned a spade. Now king of spades, spade ruff, ace of hearts (a Vienna coup), and the rest of the clubs. I was squeezed as flat as a pancake.

If I had played low on the spade lead South would have won with the king and returned a spade. Forquet wins and plays another diamond, breaking up the squeeze.

It was a vulnerable slam, not bid at the other table. We lost 13 points instead of gaining them, and the New York team won the match by 20.

That was six Lancias to the opposition, and six more went away in another match. Once again I had to take most of the blame, for this was a critical deal:

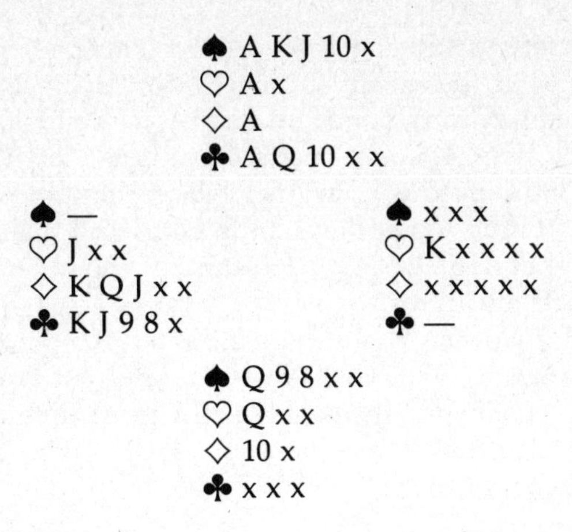

I played as South in six spades, doubled by East. A club lead surely beats the contract, but Bates (West) was content to lead the king of diamonds.

Before reading further, what do you suppose was the critical card in this contract? Remarkable as it may seem, the card that really made the difference was the 10 of diamonds!

After winning the diamond lead I drew trumps, noting West's void. Realizing that his partner had doubled because he had a void in clubs, West kept all his clubs and discarded three diamonds. Having formed the same conclusion about the club suit, I finessed dummy's 10 and cashed the ace of hearts, to arrive at this position:

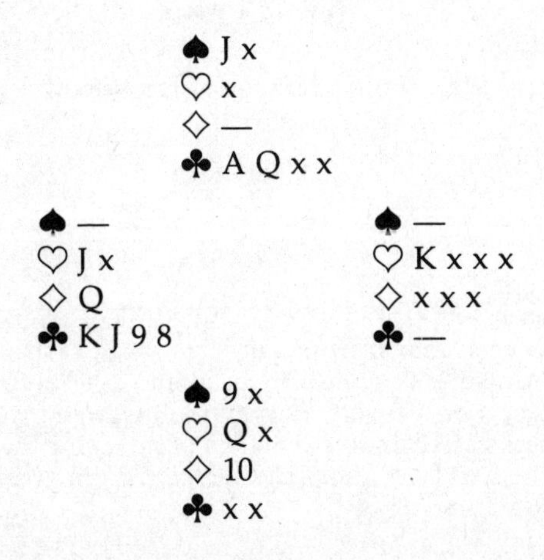

I led a small heart from dummy and Mohan (East) played low. If I go up with the queen, I make an overtrick, but another possibility entered my mind. I thought: 'If West is 0–3–5–5, as seems likely, with K x x of hearts, I must play low. Then (a) if West exits with the king of hearts I will ruff in dummy and play two more trumps, squeezing him in clubs and diamonds (the precious 10); and (b), if West exits with a diamond I will squeeze him in hearts and clubs.'

So I played a low heart, my mind full of the plaudits that would greet my analysis. But alas! West won and led the queen of diamonds. Goodbye to the squeeze and goodbye to the match!

The other deal that I remember well was played in Los Angeles against Katz and Cohen.*

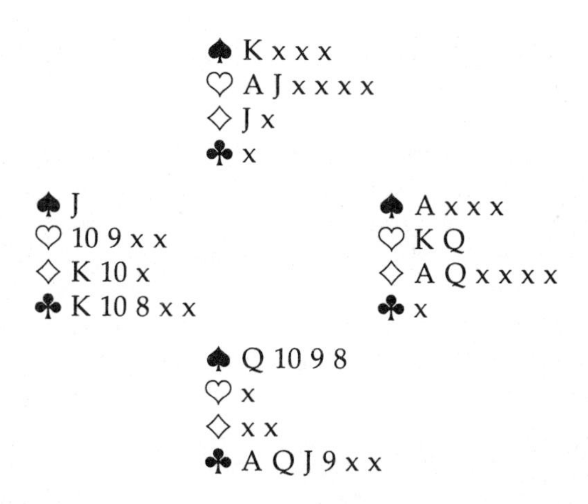

North–South were vulnerable and this was the bidding:

*This pair was later accused of exchanging illegal signals. A lawsuit followed, with vast claims. Eventually there was a fairly even-handed settlement. The insurers of the ACBL paid out 75,000 dollars to cover the legal expenses of the other side. Katz and Cohen were readmitted to the League but were barred from playing as partners for the first year. As Edgar Kaplan remarked in the *Bridge World*, the only winners from the affair were the lawyers. T.R.

South	*West*	*North*	*East*
Sharif	Cohen	Garozzo	Katz
—	—	No	1 ♢
2 ♣	dble	2 ♡	dble
2 ♠	No	No	dble
No	No	No	

I bid two spades for this reason: my partner had not opened with a weak two hearts, and the probable reason for this was that he held four spades.

West led a low diamond. After some thought Katz won with the queen and returned a club. At this point I placed him with six diamonds and a singleton club. I went up with the ace of clubs and followed with the queen. West covered and I discarded a diamond from dummy.

West switched to the jack of spades, which ran to my queen. Remembering East's double of two hearts, I placed him with 3–3–6–1 distribution, so I led a low club and ruffed in dummy, thinking that if East overruffed the remaining trumps would be 1–1. Instead, East was able to overruff and play ace and another spade, which left me a trick short. Of course, I could have made the contract. When in with the queen of spades I can ruff a diamond, play ace and another heart, and ruff a club with the king of spades.

Well, now you know how the Lancias came to present eighteen motor cars to American bridge players. You may think, from the hands I have described, that it was mostly my fault. Well, these deals were all interesting, and I must have done some good things too, because all the matches were close.

It is time, in any case, to present one of the deals played by my brilliant colleagues: this one by Belladonna who, despite his geniality and his physical resemblance to the priest in an Italian comedy, exerts such 'table presence' that his opponents are never comfortable.

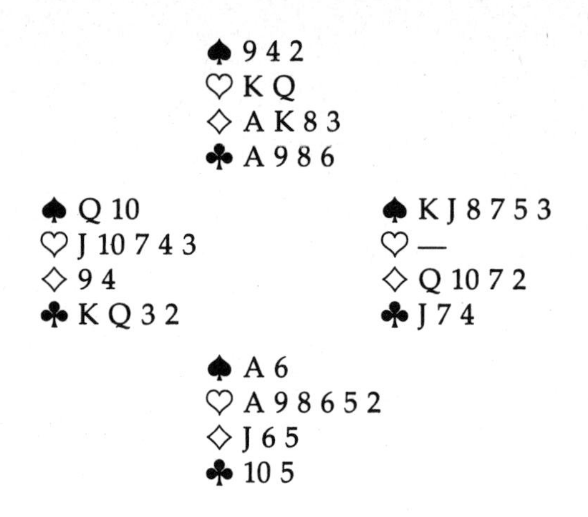

Giorgio played in four hearts. On the surface there are five losers—one in spades, two in hearts, one in diamonds, and one in clubs.

West led the king of clubs and the bridgerama commentators made their forecast: five losers, but Belladonna might save one of them by means of an endplay in the trump suit.

Declarer won with the ace of clubs and led the king of hearts, discovering the 5–0 break. He exited from dummy with a low club, won by East's jack.

East exited with a spade. Belladonna went up with the ace, crossed to the queen of hearts, and ran the 8 of clubs, discarding his second spade.

West led a spade; South ruffed, cashed two diamonds, and discarded a diamond on the 9 of clubs. Down to A 9 8 of hearts, Giorgio had no trouble in making two of the last three tricks. Four hearts made, and there was nothing the defence could have done about it.

XII

During our travels I seldom played with Giorgio Belladonna. Since he is the most difficult of opponents, it is reasonable to say that he is not the easiest of partners. He takes command of the game; he plays little tricks that are amusing but sometimes complicated. Often I find myself wondering what he wants me to do.

Is there any player who, at least once in his life, has not felt a sense of uncertainty when playing against a particular opponent? It has nothing to do with his style of play or his mannerisms. Just his presence at the table is disconcerting. He spreads a fluid that paralyses the opposition, making them incapable of playing their natural game. The opponent is like a trapeze artist in mid-air who suddenly thinks the safety net is an illusion and that he will inevitably plunge to the ground. You see, I fly through the air myself with these bold metaphors, trusting my faithful readers to extend the net.

As I say, against certain opponents I have on occasions a feeling of helplessness. I suppose that sometimes it works the other way—that my opponents are intimidated.

It is a great advantage to possess this quality. I don't believe it is possible to acquire it. Like talent, it is there or it is not. I imagine that if I sat opposite Humphrey Bogart or Orson Welles, I should feel crushed and helpless. Orson Welles especially; people with his kind of physique always make me nervous. Slim, neat players seldom affect me in that way. I am very conscious of the geometrical occupation of space. From there, it is not far to saying that stout people have an advantage in this game. An amusing idea occurs to me. Suppose a team of fat players were to play a match against a team of thin players of equal ability: who would win?

A deal that I played with Belladonna against the American champions, Goldman and Eisenberg, was extremely amusing—for some! I will show you first just the hands of North (the dummy) and East.

♠ J 10 x x
♡ A Q J x x
♢ x
♣ K x x

♡ 10 led

♠ x
♡ x x x
♢ K x x x x
♣ Q 10 x x

Goldman, South, played in four spades after his partner had opened one heart. Belladonna, West, led the 10 of hearts. Ace from dummy, a spade to the king, which holds, and a second spade, on which partner plays the ace. You discard? To be fair, you realize that partner is looking tense. Exactly what he wants is not clear, so you play safe, discarding a heart for the moment. Oh dear! This was the full hand:

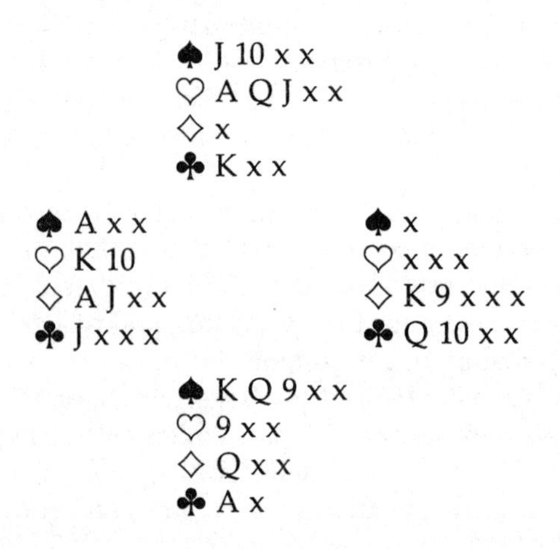

You see what you've done? You have ruined the effect of a brilliant lead that should have led to one down (king of hearts, low diamond, heart ruff) when eleven tricks were there on top. Poor Giorgio was like a balloon that has been punctured by a sharp needle!

XIII

After the great Lancia adventure I began to play bridge more regularly. The cinema had become more political, social and experimental. Films with big stars and big spectacles were succeeded by films in which actors with tortured expressions sought to convey a 'message'. In the States they still called me 'the sexiest man in the world', and in France a poll revealed that I was considered the most attractive man in the business, but the popular papers were already declaring in big headlines that I was a washed-out Casanova or, at best, a carefree charmer who was looking for new worlds to conquer.

Recently I came across the report of an interview in which I told the journalist: 'The truth is that I am about as sexy as a bus. Nevertheless, all the girls want to seduce me and find it exciting. I think I'm getting older, and those who regard me as a super-lover are living in the past.'

I had just made *The Tamarind Seed*, with Julie Andrews. I realized that it would be foolish of me to compete with the new lions of the cinema, Robert Redford, Jack Nicholson, Alan Bates and so forth.

So, to paraphrase Saint-Simon's remark about the Cardinal of Retz, I grew away from the film world as the film world grew away from me. When the newspapers referred to me, they wrote about my new enthusiasms: racing, gaming—at which, according to the gossips, I won or lost fabulous amounts—and finally bridge.

Whenever possible, I played in the *Sunday Times*, a tournament in which some of the world's best players competed, not to gain a title or reward, but just for the honour and pleasure. One of my partners in this event was Pietro Forquet. Pietro is a very different type of player from Garozzo or Belladonna. He is very careful, takes no risks, and betrays no emotion. Terence Reese, in one of his books, describes an occasion in the European Championship when Forquet, playing against France, had a misunderstanding with his partner, Siniscalco, and the pair played in 7NT doubled with a void opposite x x x in the opponents' long suit. The opponents made the first seven tricks; not a word was spoken. The French, it is said, were so dumbfounded by this superhuman display that they scarcely played a right card for the rest of the session.

This is another deal that went round the world: Forquet was playing with Garozzo against American opponents.

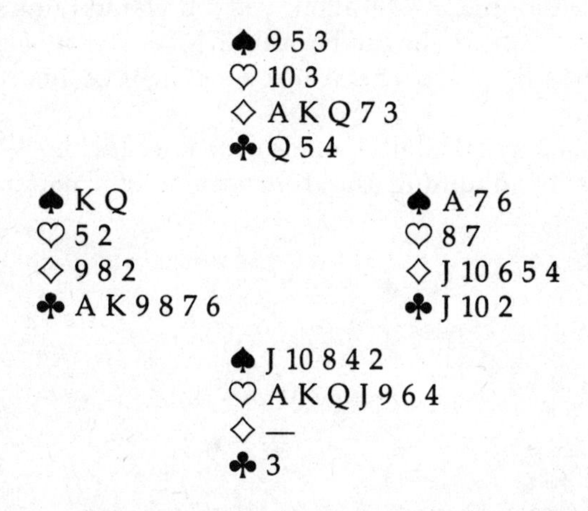

Garozzo, West, opened two clubs, Forquet responded two diamonds, and South jumped to four hearts, which was passed out.

West began with the ace of clubs and, seeing his partner's 2, switched to king of spades and queen of spades. Nine hundred and ninety-nine players out of a thousand in East's position, it is safe to say, would have followed with the other low spade, but Forquet overtook with the ace and gave his partner the ruff that was needed to beat the contract.

How did Forquet know that his partner held a doubleton, you may ask. After all, a declarer who has jumped to four hearts seldom has another five-card suit.

The answer is simple but brilliant: with K Q x or K Q x x Garozzo would have followed with a *low* spade. The hand is an example of the sort of trust that exists between two great players.

The player who has a genuine feeling for the game follows the simple line, preferring this to the kind of tortured analysis that may, on rare occasions, present a fractionally better chance. Some players will bid 'One spade, 1NT, two clubs. . . .' in the most natural and effortless manner. Others will close the fan, consult the ceiling, stroke their chins, and finally produce a laboured sequence.

Paul Chemla, who is known as the *enfant terrible* of French bridge, has extraordinary flair. His simple reasoning and direct approach enable him to play with a faultless rhythm for hour after hour. He had a normal education, yet you would think he had spent his entire life in a box at the Scala in Milan: he knows all the famous works by heart. This is just a sidelight on his complex personality.

I have been a great admirer of his ever since the day when he played this hand during the Tournament of Champions at Deauville:

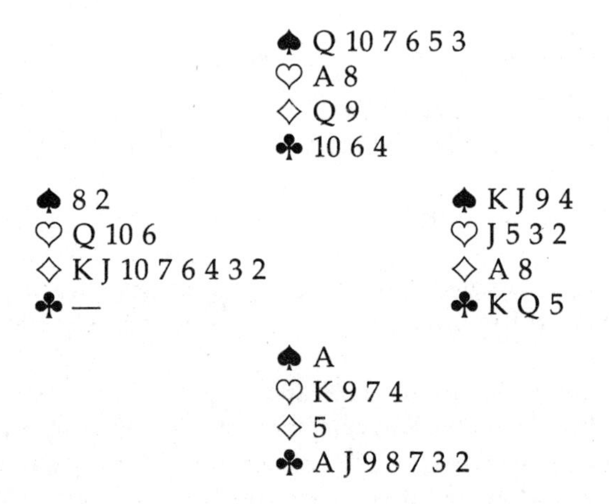

North was the dealer and the bidding went:

South	*West*	*North*	*East*
Chemla	Murray	Sharif	Kehela
—	—	No	1 ♠
2 ♣	2 ♢	3 ♣	No
5 ♣	5 ♢	No	No
5 ♡	No	6 ♣	dble
No	No	No	

Imagine that you are playing this contract of six clubs doubled. The 8 of spades is led and you win with the ace. At trick two you. . . .

Sorry, but you've missed your chance! Chemla *covered* the 8 of spades with dummy's 10 and East very naturally contributed the jack. The declarer now crossed to the ace of hearts and led the queen of spades, which was covered and ruffed. Then came king of hearts, heart ruff, 7 of spades covered and ruffed, heart ruff, and the 5 of spades, on which South was able to discard the 5 of diamonds. There was still a trump in dummy to lead through East's K Q 5. It was a brilliant coup against the pair known as 'the iron men of Canada'.

I shall never forget an occasion when Paul Chemla, myself, and two others, were trapped in a lift. All the residents of the building had gone away for the week-end; it looked as though the concierge would find us all dead on Monday morning. We were nearly asphyxiated as well, but Paul was quite unmoved. 'If I play low, what happens?' he asked us. 'He wins with the queen and. . . .'

The discussions among bridge players are not just the chatter of enthusiasts. Many hands are straightforward, but many others produce problems that can be discussed endlessly and can never be settled. For example, all American players are addicted to weak jump overcalls: they take remarkable risks to prevent opponents from exchanging information. French players don't believe in taking such risks. Both styles have their successes; there can never be a final answer.

Bridge is not an exact game, and therein lies one of its main fascinations. When you play in one of the big pairs events at

Juan-les-Pins or elsewhere, you meet a variety of opponents and you have only a few moments in which to form an opinion about their skill and their methods.

Partners, too, have their oddities. Some years ago I played with an unfamiliar partner at Juan and we had many disagreements. At one point we finished in six clubs. As the play proceeded, I discovered that he had Q x of my long suit, hearts, and had never supported me. There were fifteen tricks on top in hearts, clubs or notrumps. We were good friends, but when the session ended I pursued him along the pavement, seized him by the neck, as one seizes a cat, and said:

'But why did you pass? Why did you never support my hearts? I could kill you. . . . It reminds me of the day when I saved Rubin's life. But what happened then was worse, I agree.'

I was referring to an incident at Monte Carlo. It was all about the three of clubs. Rubin and Soloway had doubled Garozzo in four spades and had got it one down instead of three down. It was still a fair result, but on the way back to the Hôtel de Paris Rubin persisted: 'Why did you play the 3 of clubs?'

Soloway answered: 'Leave me alone. Forget it.'

Rubin: 'No. I want to know the reason. . . . Why the 3 of clubs?'

'For heaven's sake, let me alone.'

The argument continued until they reached the hotel, and Soloway began to lose his temper. He is a delightful character, very large, very easy-going. Now he took off his glasses, handed his coat to a bystander, squared his fists and lunged in Rubin's direction. I threw my arms round his waist—well, as far as I could reach—and managed to restrain him. I had saved Rubin's life, but he went on: 'All I want to know is why you played the 3 of clubs. . . .'

XIV

I have a nervous disposition, with no more control over my feelings than the Metro-Goldwyn-Mayer lion. I am very much aware of the psychological ascendancy of an opponent who has had a good result, though naturally I try to hide my feelings.

I consider it extremely important to avoid two bad boards in succession. The best plan is not to make any special effort to recover the points. Just forget the bad result and start afresh; it is silly to bear the scars of defeat like a boxer. If your opponent is clever in this respect, he will aim to press his advantage, playing with boldness and flair.

To do well at bridge, as indeed at any game, you must have a strong desire to win. Otherwise it's not worth sitting down to play. Winning does not mean solving all the problems in the game; it means simply burying your opponents.

When I lose, my good sense may tell me that I haven't played well. No matter, I tell myself, I'll do better next time. But more often I find excuses. . . . It is my partner who has played poorly. That's one of the good things about bridge: it's a partnership game, and you can always blame your partner!

You need strong nerves to play this game, and at one time I was very much lacking in control. My friends often remind me of an incident that occurred at Deauville about fifteen years ago, when I had only just begun to live in France.

One day at the Royal Hotel in Deauville I had a call from the porter's desk, informing me that M. Maurice Schumann, the

Foreign Minister, wished to speak to me. I was very impressed, especially as I did not possess French citizenship. My Minister! This could be important.

We met in the bar, and the Minister addressed me as follows: 'Monsieur Sharif, I am a very ordinary bridge player, while you, I know, are one of the greatest. It would give me exceptional pleasure to play with you.' I smiled modestly and he went on: 'I am president of a little club in Houlgate. We have a tournament on Tuesday evenings. I wonder if you could bear to play with me tonight? But I must warn you again, I am a very moderate performer. You mustn't expect any brilliancies.'

I could only reply: 'With the greatest pleasure, Minister.'

Having discussed the system we should play, we proceeded in an official car to a small club where about ten tables were situated beneath a balcony. Two impressive armchairs awaited us at Table 1, North–South.

On the first hand Maurice Schumann was the declarer in four spades. He lost three tricks early on, but the rest of his hand was high. In diamonds he had at this point A J x opposite a singleton. He led the singleton from dummy and after long consideration he inserted the jack, which lost, inevitably, to the queen. One down.

Fairly calm at this stage, I said: 'But, Minister, the contract was safe at this point. All you had to do was play the ace of diamonds.'

'Yes, but you see, I hoped that by playing the jack. . . .'

'You had ten certain tricks, but now you've gone down.'

'I thought that if. . . .'

'No matter what you thought, you had ten tricks safe.'

I took out a cigarette. I was already shaken. A few hands later we were defending and the Minister had the master trump. At one point I led the ace of spades, which my partner proceeded to ruff. This play cost two tricks and at the end of the hand I said: 'I don't understand, Minister. Why did you ruff my ace of spades with the queen of trumps?'

'Ah,' he replied. 'I wanted to be in my hand to lead a club.'

'Minister, when I play the ace of spades I want to be able to lead to the next trick. When I play a card of that sort, will you kindly allow me to continue the defence?'

A few hands later, defending against 3NT, I was unable to follow suit and signalled with the 9 of clubs. And of course he led—a spade. It was more than I could bear.

'I thought a spade was best,' he declared.

'Minister,' I said, 'when I ask you to play a spade, will you kindly do so? Just follow my lead like a little sheep. When I play the 9 of clubs, lead a club, not a spade.'

'But I thought. . . .'

I was still speaking calmly, but my temper had gone. 'Don't think,' I said. 'Just do what I ask.'

For the rest of the session I scarcely looked at my cards. At the end I threw them down and stalked off to find a taxi.

On the way back to Deauville I began to calm down and feel angry, not with the Minister, but with myself. I had wondered about it before, and now I was certain that I was completely mad. How could I be so rude to someone so charming, who had warned me he was not a serious player? I just hope that Maurice Schumann will not retain too bad a memory of his game with a bridge maniac.

XV

I am not an Egyptian with a turban, standing at the base of the pyramids. I was educated at an English school; I have considerable acquaintance with French literature; and I feel that in every way I am a Western man. I don't know whether my oriental origin has any bearing on my play. I think not. I see Japanese and Chinese players, and they play the same sort of game as anyone else. Players from the Far East may hide their feelings better, but that is the only difference. Is a Swedish tennis player different from an American tennis player? What counts is whether he plays well or not. It's the same at bridge. But whether the player is a man or a woman—that's a very different matter.

Rixi Markus, whom of course you will know, is the greatest phenomenon in women's bridge. She is the only woman I know who plays as well as a man.

Don't imagine that I am some sort of oriental pasha who judges females by their appearance and underestimates their intelligence. I greatly admire the lightness of spirit they bring to such serious matters as choosing their dresses, their coiffure, their ornaments. I am sure they are much more intelligent than men. The proof? You will never find them devoting all their time and energy to mastering so trivial a subject as bridge. They are content to play like a bird. So, how can you expect them to play as well as men?

Rixi, as I have said, is different. The first time I played with her, in a Common Market event, I broke a bridge table. Literally.

It happened on quite an ordinary hand.

The declarer was playing in three spades. Half-way through the hand the lead was in dummy, and dummy held six diamonds to the K Q 10. This suit had not been touched, and we had made three tricks.

The king of diamonds was led from dummy. Rixi played the 2. In fourth hand I won with the ace and led another suit.

The declarer ruffed, produced the jack of diamonds, and made the rest of the tricks.

As I put my cards back in the board, Rixi asked: 'Why did you take the ace of diamonds?'

'Because you played the 2. I thought you had three and the declarer a singleton.'

'That's for children.'

'No,' I said, 'it's not only for children. It's useful; it tells your opponents nothing important, and it helps your partner.'

'Nonsense!' she replied. 'I don't play with children, and I don't tell the declarer my distribution.'

'Of course not, except when it's necessary to tell your partner.'

'No, I don't play like that.'

I lost my temper completely: 'You don't play like that because you don't understand the first thing about this game.'

Instead of giving me a chance to cool down, Rixi repeated: 'You are a child.'

I stood up, banged my fist on the table—and it collapsed.

The directors appeared: change of table, and change of climate. Whatever happened, Rixi spoke just two words: 'Well played.' She also gave me the count on every occasion, whether it was important or not. All the compliments, whether justified or not, were for me like oil to a motor. The first day we had scored 54 per cent, the second day 63 per cent.

Rixi is a phenomenon. One day I heard Garozzo address her as follows: 'Rixi, it is quite possible for me to make a mistake in bidding from time to time. It is also possible for me to make a mistake in the play. On this occasion, however, I have not made a single mistake when playing the dummy. But according to you, there has not been a single hand I have played correctly.'

As Garozzo had not broken the table, she continued to criticize him. Knowing how all the cards were distributed, she told him exactly how he ought to have played.

Rixi's intensity is a vital part of her game. Away from the table she is the kindest of persons, the most loyal of friends.

On another occasion I was playing in a pairs at Gstaad with Minnie Yallouze, the wife of my friend Léon. Charming, sensitive, very timid, she speaks in a very small voice. It was not an important event, but she was nervous and on the first hand, playing with unfamiliar boards, she opened out of turn: one club.

The director was summoned. It was my very good friend, Colonel Boudrel.

'I am sorry,' he informed Minnie, 'but the rule is that your partner must pass throughout.'

He glanced at my hand, which contained 22 points, a certain slam opposite the opening bid.

'What!' I exclaimed, with a wink at the Colonel. 'I have to pass throughout? That can't be right.'

Boudrel, knowing very well what was going on, replied: 'Yes, that is so. But you, madame, may bid anything you please. You understand? You may bid as high as you like.'

It was a very friendly action, though not strictly in the best tradition of tournament direction! (As I remarked earlier, it was not a serious event.)

'Oh, very well, if that's the rule,' I said grumpily. 'You understand, Minnie?' I went on in a very emphatic tone. 'You can bid anything you like, anything. Are you sure you understand?'

'Yes, I understand.'

'Well then?'

'One club.'

XVI

It would need writers as gifted as Carlyle or Churchill to recount the history of bridge: the Culbertson–Lenz 'battle of the century', the ascendancy of the original Four Aces, the reign of Albarran in France, the championship victories of the Americans, the Italians, the British, and the French. It all began in 1925, at Balboa, a small port on the Pacific coast near the Panama canal. The millionaire Harold Vanderbilt was in quarantine, and to while away the hours he suggested some new ideas about bridge to three friends. They can hardly have imagined the way the new game would spread all over the world. Three million players in France, 20 million in the United States, and heaven knows how many there will soon be in China!

Vanderbilt introduced three new ideas: to score game or slam, you had to bid the game or slam (in Auction bridge you could play in one club, make seven and score the slam bonus); the level of the scoring was much increased; and the vulnerability factor was introduced.

The idea of a dummy was not new; it had existed since the end of the nineteenth century.

I am quite the laziest person in the world, unable even to lift the telephone to speak to the object of my adoration, but I hate to be dummy, to have no part in victory or defeat. I can bear it with a strong partner—I can relax and order a coffee. But when my partner is weak, when he hesitates and fumbles and muddles the play, I suffer tortures. I have to hide it, because otherwise he will play worse. Worst of all are the partners who know better, who are just careless. These I cannot bear.

But bridge, as they say, is a partnership game. A good relationship between the players, both technical and temperamental, is the first requirement. Two average players who are in sympathy with one another will be a stronger force than two experts who are at loggerheads. The best combination, in my opinion, is one aggressive player and one calm player who will act as a restraining influence.

I am by nature a careful, methodical player. If my partner is a great player, one of the best in the world, I am happiest if he will take the initiative, as I can trust his judgement. When my partner is about my own level, or somewhat below, I prefer to be the one who takes the risks. I apply spurs to my natural disposition and gallop to the attack.

XVII

The pairs game and the team game are very different. My own mathematical nature is better suited to the team game, which is a more balanced and rational form of contest. It calls for more concentration, more safety plays, more subtlety. But it is not as tense as the pairs game because single tricks are often unimportant.

The pairs game is a real battle because every hand has equal importance and every trick is important as well. Players must be more aggressive; they must take risks, sometimes playing for an overtrick when failure will mean one down. I must say that such hazardous procedure does not come naturally to me.

Rubber bridge is something quite different again. Psychological elements are of primary importance. You have to play a different sort of game according to the nature of your opponents. Players with good knowledge and technique are often inferior to players with good psychology.

With my love of showmanship, I am especially fond of goulashes, which are very common in France. When the bidding ends in a low part score, the contract is conceded, the cards are sorted and collected and, without any shuffling, are distributed 5–5–3. This leads, as often as not, to extraordinary freaks. If you have an eight-card suit you must be prepared for the remainder to be divided 5–0–0. Even thirteen-card suits are not all that rare. Normal bidding systems are useless, but experienced players develop certain forms of understanding.

In some ways goulashes are good training for other forms of bridge. It becomes absolutely essential to visualize the likely distribution; and it teaches the notion of sequence, in the sense that Q J 10 9 8 7 is far more reliable as a trump suit than A K x x x x. With goulashes it is playing tricks that count, not honour tricks.

The following hand has appeared in a number of French publications but may be new to English readers:

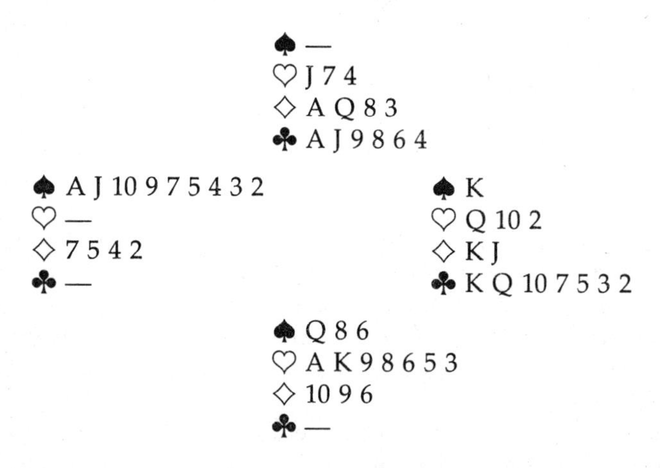

West opened four spades and North, my partner, bid 4NT, clearly for take-out. East passed and, as South, I responded six hearts. After two passes East doubled; it is seldom right, in a goulash to remove partner's double, so West passed and the hand was played in six hearts doubled.

West led the ace of spades, and I ruffed with dummy's jack of hearts, noting the fall of the spade king from East. On the 7 of hearts East played the 2; I let the 7 run, not so much because East had doubled as because West was quite likely to be void. After drawing trumps I ran the 9 of diamonds to East's jack. He exited with the king of clubs; I discarded a diamond, West threw a spade and dummy won with the ace of clubs.

At this point I claimed the contract. The opponents wanted me to play on, but experienced players will easily foresee the end position. After I had run the hearts and cashed the queen of spades (promoted on the first trick, remember), the position was:

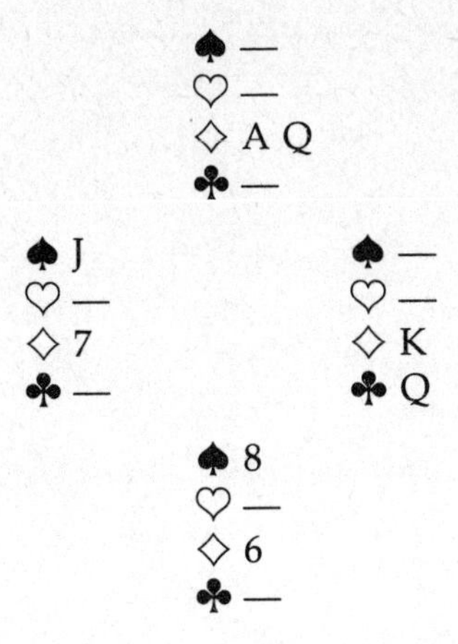

I led a diamond, and when West followed with the 7 I knew the king would fall on my right because West's last card was known to be a spade. It is the type of play known as a show-up squeeze.

At the Club Albarran a group of us played goulashes every day for ten years, and there were many remarkable incidents. The most extraordinary, perhaps, occurred when a player named Klahr held what I will call the West cards.

South opened 1NT, which in a goulash means that you have some good cards but no long suit, West doubled, and North redoubled. All passed and the hand was played in 1NT redoubled.

Klahr, who was on lead, took out a cigarette and said to the others: 'Sorry, I must think for a little while.' Finally, he placed the 3 of clubs on the table. North was void of clubs; East was void of clubs; South followed suit with the 2. 'Oh, good, they break,' exclaimed Klahr, who had led twelfth best from a twelve-card suit!

Hands I Remember

XVIII

Like some Casanova who produces a packet of love-letters as evidence of his adventures, I propose, for the remainder of this book, to describe some of the most remarkable deals I have encountered during the last twenty years.

Some recall my old Egyptian playmates, others the time of the Circus, when my partners were the famous Italians. I pay tribute also to the Dallas Aces, my favourite opponents, and to the French team that was victorious in the 1980 Olympiad. And for those whose interest lies especially in complicated problems, I add one or two deals of that sort.

I begin with some hands that go back to the time when my friends from Egypt and myself were known as the 'Wild Ones'. I should add, perhaps, that I may have given a slightly false picture; adventurous we may have been, but we all knew the game pretty well.

In a duplicate at the Élysée in Paris, where I caught up with my friends from the old days, I picked up the following hand:

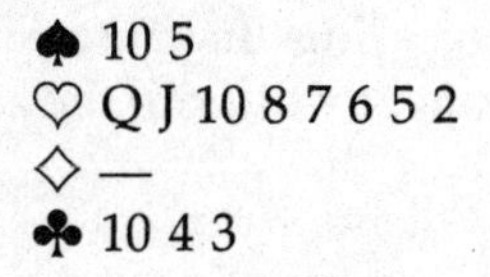

Neither side was vulnerable, and East, on my right, opened one diamond. Jumping in at the deep end, I overcalled with four hearts. West doubled and all passed. West led a club and I surveyed:

♠ A J 6
♡ A 9 3
◇ J 6 5 2
♣ Q 7 5

♣ 2 led

♠ 10 5
♡ Q J 10 8 7 6 5 2
◇ —
♣ 10 4 3

I played low from dummy, and East won with the king. Two thoughts went through my mind at this point. One was that quite possibly there was no game for the opposition; the other, that it seemed a little odd for West to lead a club from J x x or J x x x instead of his partner's suit. He might hold something like A x or A x x in diamonds and be afraid of leading up to the king.

East returned the king of diamonds. I ruffed with the 5 of hearts and led the 6, on which West played low. Expecting him to hold the guarded king, I finessed the 9, which held; East discarded a diamond.

Things looked better now. There were nine tricks on top and possibilities in spades and clubs, at any rate in combination. I crossed to the ace of hearts, ruffed another diamond, on which West's ace appeared, and led the 10 of spades. It was fairly certain that West would hold one of the honours; he would not have doubled four hearts on the strength of the ace of diamonds and K x of hearts. Looking a little uncomfortable, West covered the 10 of spades with the king. I won with the ace, and the position was then:

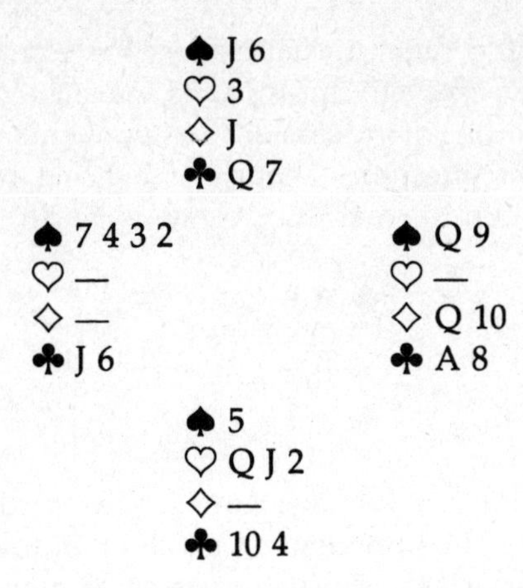

I led the jack of diamonds from dummy, and East played the queen. Now I discarded my last spade, and East, as you will see, was end-played. A diamond or a club is obviously fatal, and if he tries the queen of spades I can ruff high and cross to the 3 of hearts to make the jack of spades. The full hand was:

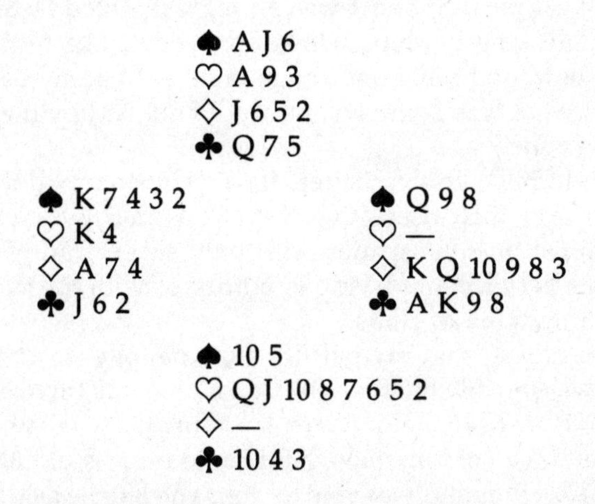

One of my favourite partners is Georges Gresh. He is a first-class player but like many others he has certain maddening habits. For example, his main objective always is to arrive at 3NT. In pursuit of this aim, he pays no attention whatsoever to his partner's frantic sign-offs, or indeed to anything else that is happening around him. I could recount many examples of this tendency but will content myself by describing an incident that took place some years ago during a big tournament in Spain.

Since the beginning of the session our opponents had kept up a steady stream of questions about our bidding methods. My patience had begun to wear thin when, as North, I picked up:

♠ A K Q 6
♡ Q 8 6
◇ 10 7 5
♣ K 3 2

We were playing a natural system with five-card majors, so I opened one club. The opponent on my left put down his cards, removed his spectacles and began a searching inquiry. Was one club conventional? he asked. How many clubs did it show? It must have been obvious to anyone on the far side of the room that this player held long clubs himself, but not, apparently, to Gresh, who was studying his own cards. When East finally passed, after a significant look in the direction of his partner, Gresh bid one heart. West passed, and I was strongly tempted to bid 1NT to protect my king of clubs. However, I don't like to make anti-system bids, so I rebid one spade, trusting that my partner had realized what was going on and would not occupy the notrump stand.

I should have known better. '1NT,' Gresh announced.

Furious at this insensitive display, I tried two spades. We might finish in four spades with only seven trumps, but that would be better than playing in notrumps with the lead coming through my king of clubs.

'Three clubs,' said my partner quite happily.

This was too much. I thought for a moment of three hearts, but it would have been madness to play in hearts, with West holding a singleton or void in clubs. All I could do was bid 3NT.

West, as I thought, was void in clubs and led the jack of spades. This was the full hand:

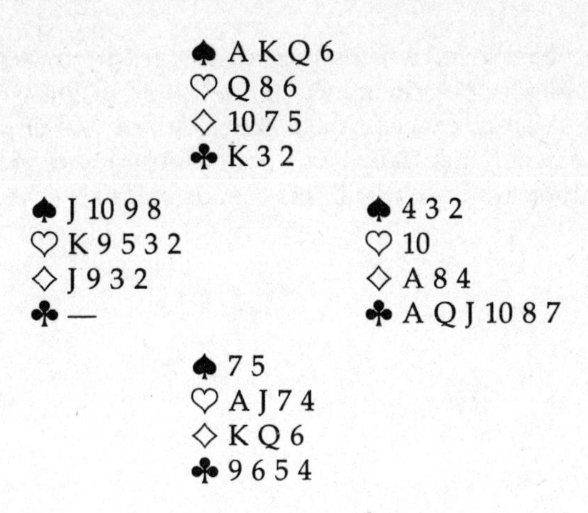

Gresh won with the queen of spades in dummy and led a diamond to the king. Returning to dummy with the king of spades, he tried a finesse of the jack of hearts. West won and led a third round of spades, South discarding a club. East captured the next diamond and exited with a diamond. This left:

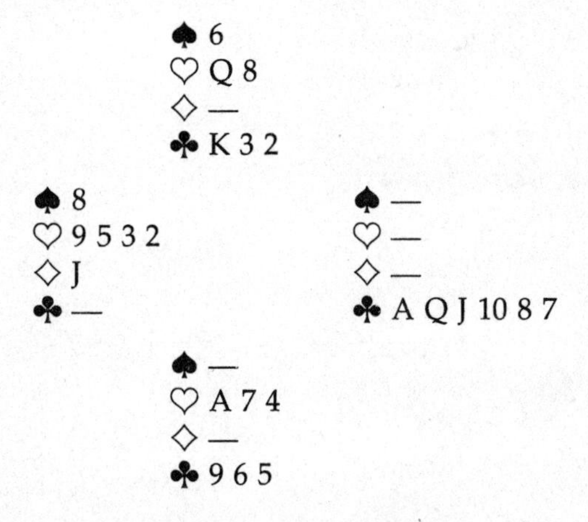

South had lost two tricks so far. Having concluded by now that East's questions were based on a long suit of clubs, he had an exact picture of the remaining cards. He began by finessing the 8 of hearts; then he led a low club from the table, East winning with the 10. If East now plays ace and another club, West is squeezed, and in practice East played well, exiting with the jack of clubs.

West, meanwhile, was obliged to throw his master diamond. Gresh then cashed the queen of hearts and exited with a spade, forcing West to concede the last trick to the ace of hearts.

My partner, naturally, was both amused and pleased. All I could think was: what will this cost us before the session ends?

XIX

The textbooks say that in match play it is wrong to bid a grand slam unless you can virtually count thirteen tricks. Much depends, surely, on the state of the match. When the following deal occurred in a 'Patton' my team was meeting its closest rivals and we felt we were behind, so it was not unreasonable to take the big chance. Paul Chemla was North, and we held these cards:

♠ A Q J 10 8 7 6
♡ 8 2
◇ Q 6
♣ A K

♠ 2 led

♠ K 9 5
♡ A K 9 5
◇ A 10
♣ J 9 6 4

We were playing a 16–18 notrump, as is usual in France, but I felt that my good intermediates justified a 1NT opening. My partner bid three spades, forcing. Perhaps I should have bid a cautious 3NT, or four spades, but I liked the look of my hand, as they say, and I showed my lowest control, four diamonds. We soon finished in 7NT. Seven spades would have been slightly better, perhaps, but Paul was influenced by his 7–2–2–2 shape and the possibility of a red-suit lead.

West led a spade, taking no chances, and it was clear that we had only twelve tricks on top. There were a number of possibilities. For example, if East held the queen of clubs and West the king of diamonds I could make the contract with a double squeeze (play off the ace of diamonds and the top clubs, then run all the spades; East would have to unguard hearts to keep the queen of clubs, and then West would be squeezed between hearts and the king of diamonds). Alternatively, there might be a simple squeeze against East in the minor suits.

Retaining all my chances, I played off six rounds of spades, discarding a heart, a club and the 10 of diamonds from my own hand. While this was going on, East discarded clubs and diamonds quite happily, while West was showing evident signs of strain, finally parting with a heart. I formed the opinion that West was guarding the minor suits, East the hearts; so be it, I must change my plan and aim to squeeze West in the minors.

Instead of releasing the ace of diamonds, as I had originally intended, I cashed the top hearts and returned to dummy with a club. The position then was:

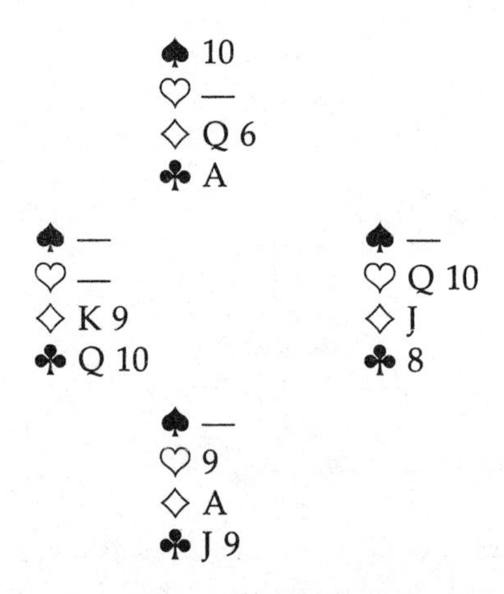

On the 10 of spades I discarded my heart and West's discomfort was very easy to observe. The full hand was something like this:

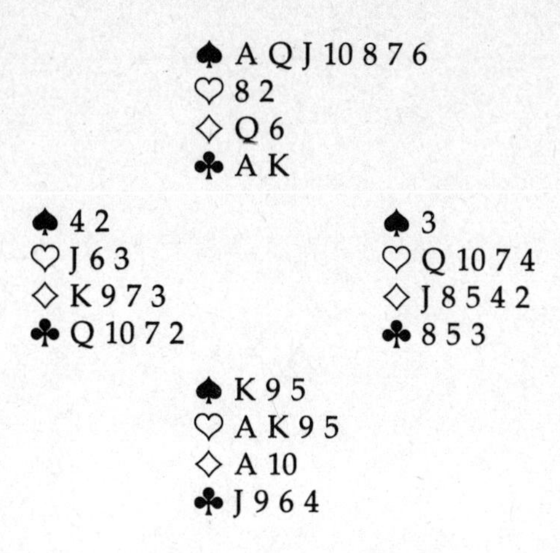

The ending was a criss-cross squeeze. This type of squeeze occurs when the top controls, the A K of clubs in this instance, are isolated—not supported by a lower card. Two points arise: one, that on such hands the declarer should not make an early decision to play for a particular type of squeeze; two, that when a squeeze is threatened the defenders must aim to give nothing away by the manner in which they play their cards; often it is good tactics to unguard an honour quite early in the play.

XX

My friend Léon Yallouze* is always capable of playing very good bridge and sometimes, if the moon is in the right place, great bridge. Nevertheless, when we play together we usually have two or three disasters. These are due partly to his idiosyncratic style and partly to my inability to draw the right conclusions.

And that's not all. Léon has one habit that I find rather tiresome: he is always asking opponents about their systems and conventions, almost as though he intended to take them up himself. There was an occasion when opponents reached 3NT after this bidding:

South	*North*
1 ♣	1 ♢
2NT	3NT
No	

Léon led the king of hearts and this is what I could see:

*Léon, I am sorry to say, died in the year that this book appeared. He was a martyr to asthma. T.R.

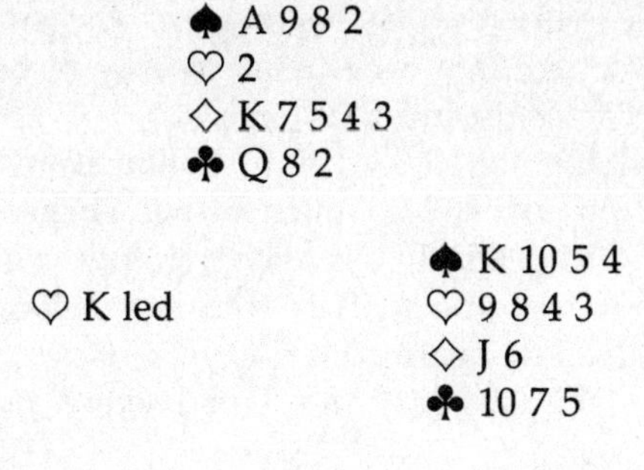

On the king of hearts I signalled with the 8 and declarer played the 5. Léon now turned to the dummy and inquired whether South could have four cards in a major suit. 'Yes,' replied North. West then followed with the queen of hearts. South won with the ace and ran the queen of spades to my king.

At this point, what conclusions would you draw? With K Q J x x in hearts Léon would have no reason to ask any questions; he would read my 8 as a signal from four small and would naturally continue with the queen or jack. In all probability he held K Q J x; it therefore occurred to me to return the *low* heart; if by chance the declarer played the 10, I would regain the lead and play a club. Sadly, the full hand was:

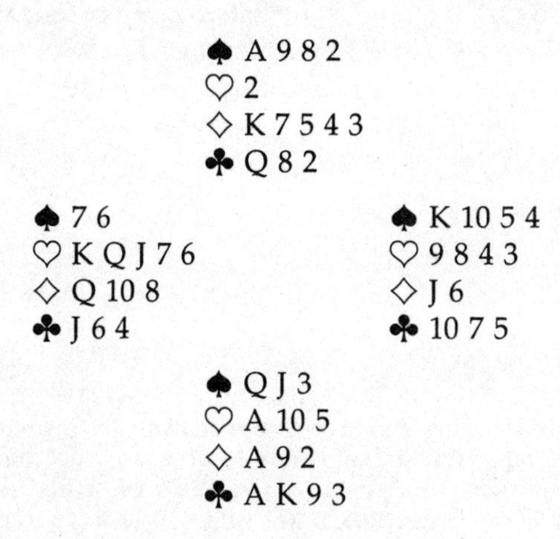

As a result of my play the hearts were blocked and South had no difficulty in landing nine tricks by way of two spades, one heart, two diamonds and four clubs.

The discussion that I had with Yallouze at the end of the tournament did not carry us much farther. I began by demanding what had induced him to ask such a pointless question.

He answered in effect: 'It is true that I could hardly have followed with a low heart from K Q J x x. However, I wanted to understand their system, and I had every right to put the question.'

Oh, quite! He wanted to know, if I understand correctly, whether the opponent might theoretically possess a holding that could hardly exist in the present case.*

Léon and I had our successes too. I am glad I didn't let him down on this deal, where in fourth position I held:

♠ J 10 4 2
♡ 7 6 3
◇ J 5 2
♣ A 5 3

West, who was vulnerable, opened three diamonds; double by my partner, pass by East. My hand might have been worse, it is true, but I thought it would be foolish to jump to four spades. So I bid simply three spades, and partner raised to four. West led the 10 of hearts and I contemplated these two hands:

*Something, I feel, is wrong with the analysis of this hand; perhaps Omar recollected a similar deal and did not reconstruct it accurately. If South (as Omar supposed) had held A 10 x x of hearts he would not have won the second trick; also, how could East expect to regain the lead with the 9 of hearts? One further point is not without interest: it is not, according to the Proprieties, correct to act on an inference drawn from partner's question. T.R.

♠ A K Q 9 5
♡ A K J 5
♢ 3
♣ 9 4 2

♡ 10 led

♠ J 10 4 2
♡ 7 6 3
♢ J 5 2
♣ A 5 3

My first thought was that the 10 of hearts might well be a singleton. In that case a good plan would be to eliminate the diamonds; then, when I exited with the second round of clubs, the opponents would be helpless. West would be forced to concede a ruff and discard; East would be forced to lead into the tenace.

I was pleased to see the trumps fall in two rounds. When I led a diamond from dummy, East played the king; West overtook and led the 8 of hearts. Interesting! My original diagnosis—that West held a singleton heart—was evidently wrong. As for the diamonds, it looked as though East's king was a singleton. He would have played low from K x, hoping that his partner would win and lead a second heart.

The plot was beginning to thicken. If West held eight diamonds, two spades and two hearts, how many clubs did that leave him? A singleton, obviously.

It looked as though—for the first time in my career, incidentally—I had a chance to execute a double ruff-and-discard elimination. The first move was to cash the ace of clubs, on which West dropped the queen. Then I led the jack of diamonds; West covered and was allowed to hold the trick. When East showed out, I knew I was on the right track. The position after this trick was:

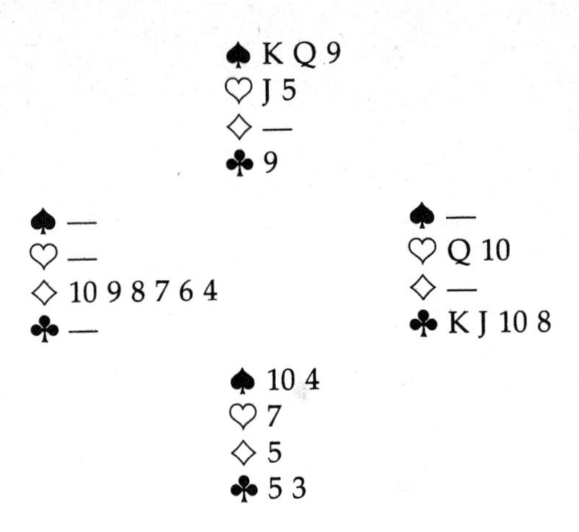

West led the 10 of diamonds and I discarded the last club from dummy; on the next diamond I ruffed in dummy and disposed of my losing heart. I had lost just three tricks, all in diamonds.

XXI

In my early days as a tournament player my favourite partner was Pierre Schemeil, a most colourful character who has achieved the remarkable feat of representing five different countries in international competition—a record that will surely never be equalled. Some of his ideas have had a great influence on French players, notably in the domain of sputnik doubles and bids with different meanings, such as the multicoloured two diamonds. Nowadays he devotes himself to the difficult task of captaining the French international team, which won the 1980 Olympiad, and to writing numerous articles on the game.

Whenever I run into him I manage to extract the story of his latest calamity in a pairs event. This is always enjoyable because, as you will have guessed, he is one of those specialists in the pairs game who thinks that events can be won only by acrobatics that would have no place in any other form of bridge.

It would be unkind, and untrue, to say that these acrobatics were never successful. But when they fail the result is often most amusing. His partner on the following deal was Jean Calix.

♡ 3 led

♠ K J 7
♡ A 7 6 4
◇ 6 5
♣ A 9 4 3

Pierre, who favours a weak notrump in pairs play, opened 1NT as South and North raised to 3NT. The unknown opponent in the West seat led a low heart. Schemeil went up with the king in dummy—and led a low spade to the jack. West won with the queen and switched to a low diamond from what turned out to be A x x. The 9 lost to the jack, a diamond was returned, and in no time the contract was defeated by two tricks.

I dare say that many of my readers, sitting in North's position, would have ventured a word of criticism. 'Partner,' they might have said, 'dear partner, can you not count? You had nine tricks on top—five clubs and two ace–kings.'

But Jean Calix, who knows the game—and knows his partner—said simply, 'Well played, partner.'

The eternal kibitzer had another question: 'Monsieur Schemeil, please excuse me if I am wrong, but since the clubs were breaking 3–1, might you not possibly have made this contract?'

Let us consider the matter seriously. Was South in any way justified in taking this risk for the sake of a possible extra trick?

The answer is yes! In the long run such play would bring in a large number of match points.

Almost every North–South pair is going to finish in 3NT. Unless diamonds are led, and the suit is divided in a particular way, every pair is going to make at least nine tricks. To make just nine tricks may well be a below average result. And how likely is it that the early spade finesse will cost the contract? Consider these possibilities:

1. The spade finesse may win.

2. Even if it loses, the odds are that West will continue hearts. As it turned out, East held Q 10 x and had played low on the first trick.

3. If West held K x x of diamonds, instead of A x x, he would be much less inclined to attack diamonds. (It is true that West should be able to place declarer with K J of spades, ace of hearts, and, since he had not begun to develop the suit, ace of clubs; there would therefore not be room for the ace of diamonds as well, but average players don't make this kind of calculation.)

4. It would not occur to most defenders that the declarer would take an early, very dangerous, finesse when he had nine tricks on top. South *ought* to have at least the jack of diamonds.

So the fatal switch to diamonds was very unlikely. You may say, why not run the clubs and then decide whether it will be safe to take the spade finesse? The answer to this is that, as the hand progressed, the situation would become clearer to the defenders and it might become too dangerous to take the spade finesse. At least, that would be Pierre's answer. Shall we leave it by saying that only an imaginative expert or a complete mug would finesse the spade at trick two?

Here is a deal from the French trials some years ago that had the whole country arguing and analysing—the 20,000-odd tournament players, anyway. I warn you, it is difficult, but it has some instructive features.

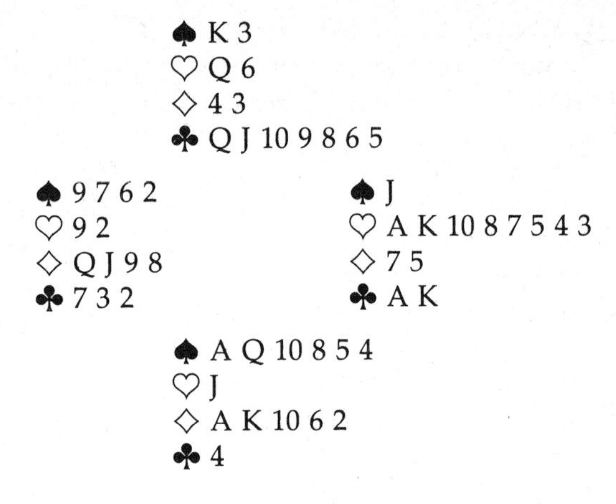

At one table East played in five hearts doubled, one down. At the other table East decided to take his chance against four spades. The declarer was the popular international, Henri Svarc.

The defence began with two rounds of hearts. South ruffed, played the two top diamonds, and ruffed the third diamond with the king of spades. With the spades 4–1 and the diamonds not yet established, he had to lose a trick in each suit.

The vultures, who from their great height could see all four hands, swooped on this deal with avidity. 'Henri should have made it,' declared some of the experts. 'Don't ruff the second heart: discard a club. If East leads a third heart, ruff with the spade 10 and discard a diamond from dummy. After ace and another diamond, ruff a club and ruff the next diamond with the king of spades. Come back to hand with another club ruff, cash ace of spades, then lead the master diamonds. West ruffs the last diamond but must then play from 9 7 of spades into declarer's Q 8.'

A double-dummy line, I consider, and not even exact. Do you see why? It is not at all obvious. East can discard his second club when the third diamond is ruffed; then he ruffs a club with the jack of spades, promoting an extra trump trick for his partner.

So, what is better? Try ruffing the second heart and leading a *club* at once. This is good technique, establishing communication. If East returns a diamond or a club or a trump, South can succeed quite easily, losing just a diamond, a club and a heart. The best defence is a heart.

Now comes a critical play: South must discard a diamond. West has two alternatives and we must consider them both.

(a) *West discards a club.* South ruffs in dummy with the 3 of spades, ruffs a club low, and plays three rounds of diamonds, ruffing with the spade king. Now a club from dummy, and whether or not East ruffs at this point with the jack of spades, West is end-played in the manner described above.

(b) *West ruffs the third heart with the 6 of spades.* Dummy does not overruff, but throws a diamond. There is no defence now. Whatever West plays, a round of trumps is drawn with the king, a club is ruffed, and a diamond is ruffed with the 3 of spades. A club is cashed and the next club is ruffed with the 10 of spades. West makes only one more trick.

A difficult hand, as I said, but note the technique, especially the early club from South, the third heart from East and, in the second sequence, the diamond discard from dummy.

XXII

Four hearts made at one table, six down at the other! That was the remarkable result on this deal from the match between France and North America in the 1974 Bermuda Bowl:

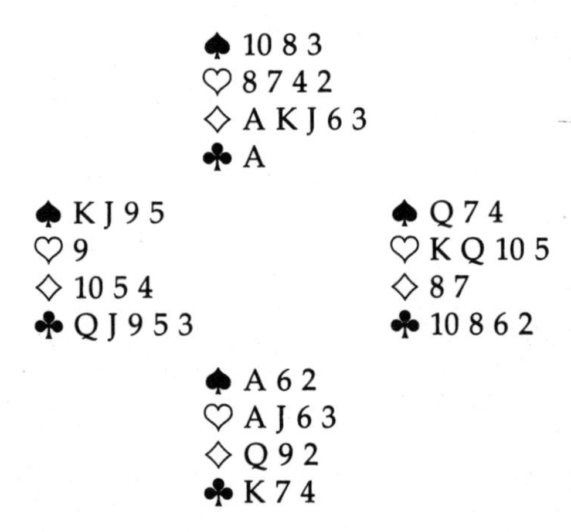

In the closed room the French West led the queen of clubs. Bob Hamman won in dummy, led a low heart to the ace, and ruffed a club. The next heart was won by the queen and West discarded a club. It would have been wiser to signal with the 9 of spades, for East, nervous of opening up the spades, now led a club. South won, entered dummy with a diamond, and led a heart from the table. East won and the defence cashed a trick in clubs—but that was all.

At the other table Boulenger received the more dangerous lead of a low spade. He now staked everything on a 3–2 break in hearts. Winning the first trick, he led a club to the ace, returned to the ace of hearts, and discarded a spade on the king of clubs. He could have saved a few tricks now by crossing to dummy for the next trump lead, but instead he played a trump from hand, hoping to lose just one spade and two hearts. Calamity! East pulled all the trumps; West discarded his diamonds; and the defenders made the rest of the tricks.

West's opening lead of a low spade may seem to have been an inspired guess, but compare the bidding at the two tables.

Closed room

South	*West*	*North*	*East*
Hamman	Lebel	Wolff	Mari
1 ♡	No	2 ♢	No
2NT	No	4 ♡	No
No	No		

Now a club is the natural lead for West.

Open room

South	*West*	*North*	*East*
Boulenger	Goldman	Svarc	Blumenthal
1 ♣	No	1 ♢	No
1 ♡	No	4 ♡	No
No	No		

The prepared opening of one club was unlucky: it pointed the way to a spade lead.

You may think it surprising that two pairs in a world championship should miss the safer contract of 3NT. In general, players tend to finish in the major suit when they have discovered a 4–4 fit and at least one of the hands is unbalanced.

However, Belladonna and Garozzo managed it in another match. This was their bidding:

South	*North*
Belladonna	Garozzo
1NT(1)	2 ♣
2 ◇(2)	2NT(3)
3NT(4)	No(5)

(1) 13–15 balanced.
(2) Showing four hearts.
(3) Asking for distribution.
(4) Showing 4–3–3–3.
(5) In view of his strong diamonds and weak hearts, he prefers to play in notrumps.

A very sophisticated auction, I am sure you will agree.

Michel Lebel was on the losing side on the deal I have just described, but now he is an Olympic champion and recognized as one of the two or three best players in France. The following deal was played during the French trials one year.

♠ 10
♡ J 9 6
◇ J 9 6 5
♣ K Q 8 7 6

♠ 2 led

♠ K J 6
♡ K Q 7 4
◇ A Q 7
♣ A J 5

South plays in 3NT and West leads the 2 of spades (third or fifth best, in accordance with the French style). Dummy's 10 holds the trick. How do you proceed?

It looks as though West has led from A Q x x x in spades. If you play on hearts, and East has the ace, you will be down at once. You could cash the clubs, but this will give East the chance to signal in hearts (assuming he has the ace), and the defence will be easy.

It is slightly better to play on diamonds. If the finesse loses and West leads a heart, you will be defeated, but your play will have cost only one trick. And it is not certain that West will find the best defence. If he has a doubleton club, for example, he may think that his partner has a guard.

Lebel led a diamond to the queen, therefore, which held. Then he played off five rounds of clubs. It is time now to show you the full deal.

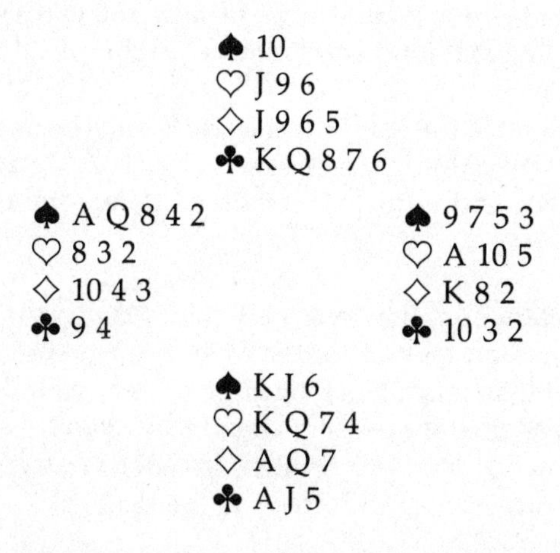

Spade to the 10, diamond finesse, five rounds of clubs. West had to make three discards. He must keep all his spades, obviously, and it is dangerous to bare the 10 of diamonds because the declarer will probably lead the jack on the next round; so West discarded three hearts. This left:

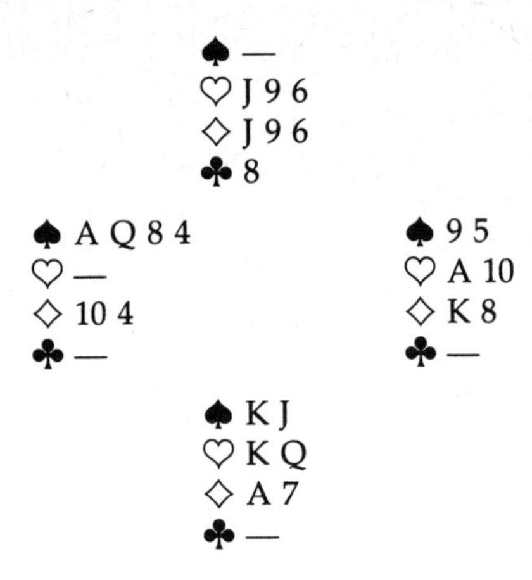

South led the jack of diamonds from dummy, covered by the king and ace. With a picture now of how the cards lay, Lebel exited with a low diamond and West had to concede a trick to the king of spades.

At the other table the lead was the same, and the declarer tried the 9 of hearts from dummy at the second trick. East smartly went up with the ace and returned a spade to defeat the contract.

I described, earlier on, the occasion when, playing for the Circus against a Canadian team, I underled an ace against a slam and scored a notable success. Not long after, at Deauville, I attempted a similar play against the excellent pair from Taiwan, V. Shen and C. S. Shen, who, like two Smiths, are not related. We were playing on bridgerama, and this was the deal:

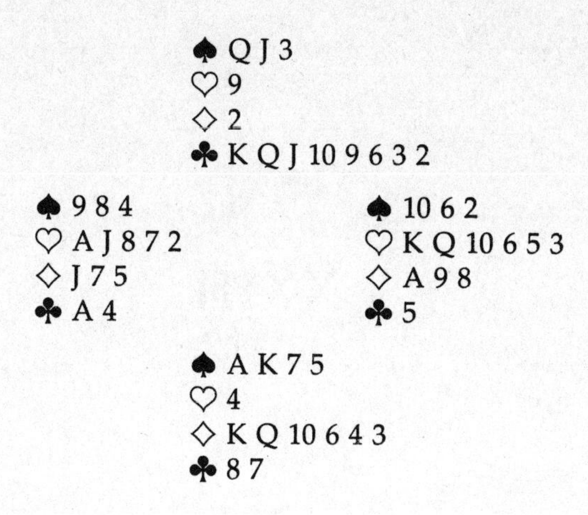

I was West and the bidding went:

South	*West*	*North*	*East*
1 ♢	1 ♡	2 ♣	4 ♡
4 ♠	No	No	No

South's four spades, I must say, looks unsound to me: the Chinese players are certainly not lacking in enterprise.

My hand, with the three spades and three diamonds, did not look at all promising in defence. This induced me to find the 'brilliant' lead of the 4 of clubs!

Dummy's 9 won the trick and the Chinaman allowed himself a slight look of surprise. A second round of clubs ran to my ace. The only chance now was to weaken the dummy, so I led ace of hearts and followed with a second heart. If South accepts the force and plays for trumps to be 3–3, he makes the rest of the tricks, but the declarer could hardly believe in such good fortune. He ruffed in dummy and led a diamond from the table, no doubt intending to finesse the 10. But alas, my partner went up with the ace and led another heart ('I was following your defence,' he said afterwards, displaying the traditional tendency of experts to blame their partners). This time the declarer could hardly refuse the gift. He ruffed in hand, drew trumps and made the rest of the tricks.

I ran to the window, intending to throw myself out, but I had forgotten—we were on the ground floor!

XXIII

After the Egyptians and the French, back to the Italians. I have written about them already, but the subject is inexhaustible. Some of the deals I shall be describing are well-known; others are new. First, a hand played by Garozzo in a pairs tournament:

♠ K J 10 8
♡ J
◇ Q 10 9 6 5 4 3 2
♣ —

♣ K led

♠ A 9 6 3 2
♡ A 8 3 2
◇ A 7
♣ 10 9

Garozzo and Belladonna reached six spades as follows:

South	*West*	*North*	*East*
1 ♠	dble	4 ♣	5 ♣
dble	No	5 ♡	dble
redble	No	6 ♠	No
No	No		

North's four clubs showed strong support for spades and a control in clubs. Five hearts showed a further control, in hearts. South's redouble promised the aces of both red suits. Neat, but when West led the king of clubs the contract was far from laydown.

A small test: what do you suppose was the declarer's first play after he had ruffed the opening lead with the 10 of spades?

It is not too difficult when posed as a problem, but it was a nerve-racking play to make at the table. Benito's first move was to lead the jack of spades from dummy and let it run. When all followed, he played a diamond to the ace and returned a diamond, won by West, who led another club. This reduced the dummy to a singleton king of spades, but the declarer was in control, as you will see when you look at the full hand:

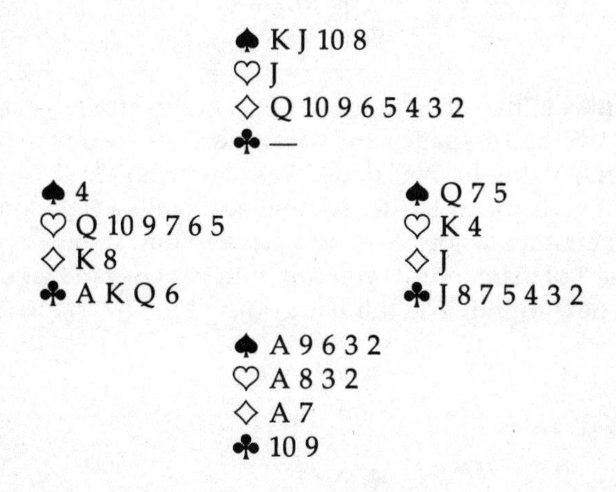

The play so far has been: club ruffed with the spade 10; jack of spades, winning; ace of diamonds, diamond to the king, club ruffed with the 8 of spades. The declarer still has to decide whether West began with a singleton or doubleton spade. It seems to me that West could have been 2–5–2–4, but Benito pursued his original idea and led diamonds from the table. As soon as East ruffed he was overruffed, and dummy was high after a spade to the king.

Pietro Forquet is certainly capable of brilliant play, but the outstanding feature of his game is his steadiness and consistency.

This deal from a pairs event is typical; the play he made, in a technical sense, was extremely simple, yet it was missed by all the other players in the same contract.

♠ K Q 8 4 2
♡ 3
♢ Q J 8 5
♣ A Q 7

♠ 3 led

♠ J
♡ A K Q 8 7 5
♢ K 10 7 6 2
♣ K

You play in five diamonds after East has overcalled in spades. West leads the 3 of spades to the ace, and a low spade comes back. You ruff with the 10. Well done! West discards a club. You follow with a low diamond to the jack and ace. Not so well done! East returns another spade. Now you have to guess: either you ruff with the 7 of diamonds or you ruff with the king and take a view on the next round. The full hand was:

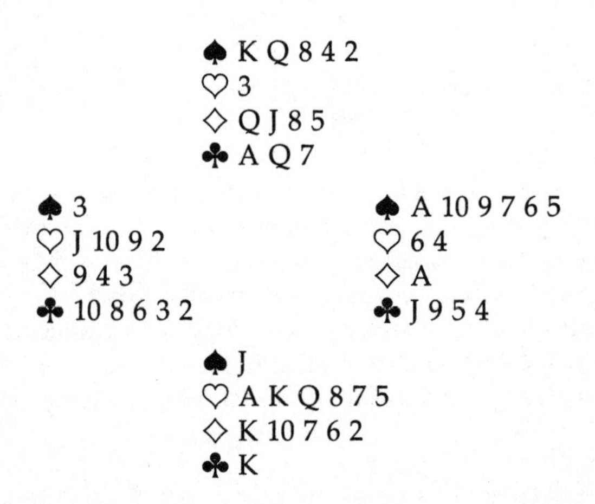

When Forquet played the hand he did not need to guess at all.

After ruffing the second spade with the diamond 10, he crossed to the ace of clubs and led the first round of trumps from dummy. East played the ace and followed with a low spade. Now Forquet was able to ruff with the king and pick up the remaining trumps without any need to guess.

I propose now to describe quite briefly two hands that will not be new to assiduous readers of bridge literature. Italian mythology attributes the first to Forquet, the second to Belladonna. These great players say, 'Well, perhaps I remember something like it.' If you have seen these hands before, you may like to read on quickly; if not, you will enjoy them.

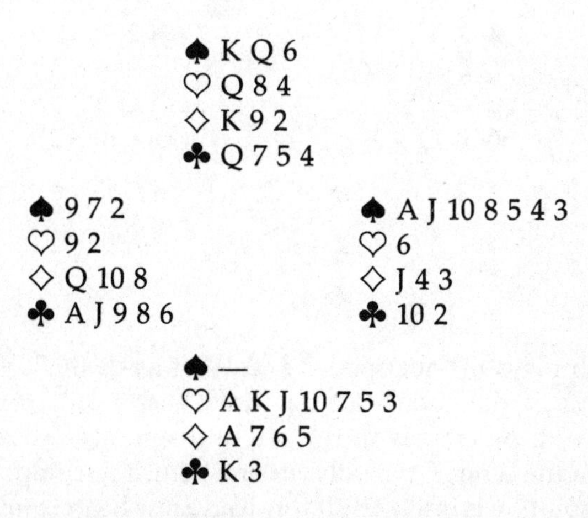

South plays in six hearts after East has opened with a pre-emptive three spades and has been supported by his partner.

West leads the 2 of spades (correct from three small when the card is evidently not a singleton). What should happen? There are three interesting possibilities.

1. The queen of spades is headed by the ace and South ruffs. After drawing two rounds of trumps he leads a low club from hand. The defence is helpless. If West plays the ace, declarer has two diamond discards, one on the queen of clubs, one on the king of spades. If West ducks, the declarer wins with the queen of clubs, discards the king of clubs on the king of spades and loses just a diamond.

2. When South plays the queen of spades on the first trick, East, knowing that the declarer is void, plays low. The declarer is forced to take a premature discard and cannot succeed.

3. South plays *low* from dummy on the opening lead. East plays the 10 and South ruffs. After drawing trumps he leads the low club, as before. Now, if West plays the ace, two discards can be established; and if West ducks, he loses his club trick.

The second deal:

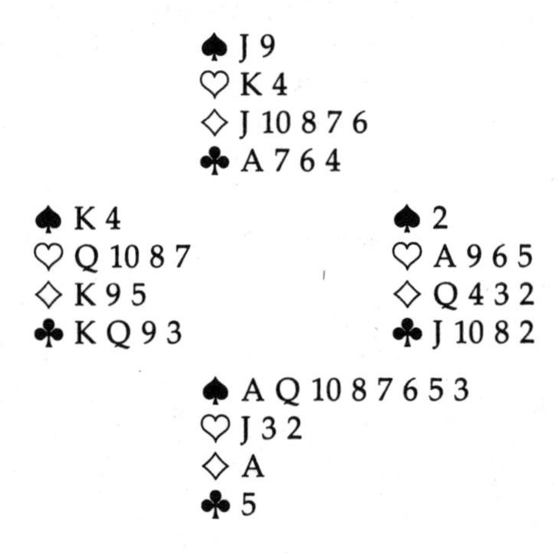

South plays in four spades and West leads the king of clubs. South is in danger of losing three hearts and a spade. For example, if he crosses to the ace of diamonds and leads a low heart to the king, East will win and return a trump.

The solution is brilliant: simply lead a low heart from dummy at trick two. West heads the jack with the queen but has no defence. He can play a heart to the ace and his partner will return a spade, but South, of course, will go up with the ace and make sure of his heart ruff.

The partnership of Giorgio Belladonna and Walter Avarelli, playing the Roman Club, was for many years the backbone of the Italian team. This deal from the Italy–US match in 1959 may be said to uphold the proposition that great players are lucky players.

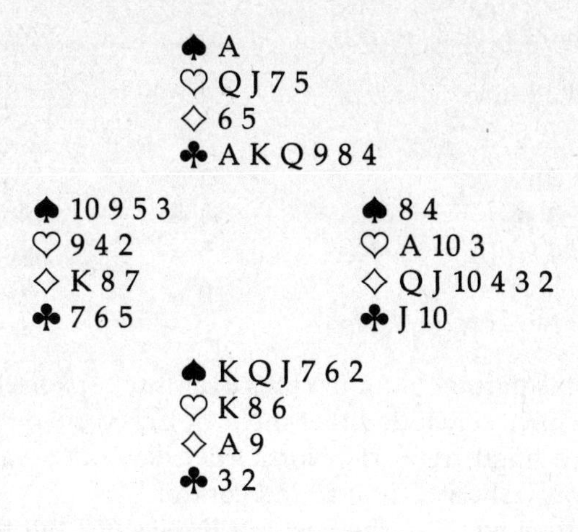

Playing in clubs or spades, the declarer appears to have twelve tricks—thirteen without a heart lead—but after a diamond opening there is an unfortunate and insuperable block in either contract. The American audience watching on bridgerama was relieved when Fishbein and Hazen stopped short with this auction:

South	*West*	*North*	*East*
—	—	—	No
1 ♠	No	2 ♣	No
2 ♠	No	3 ♡	No
3 ♠	No	4 ♠	No
No	No		

West led a diamond and South made eleven tricks for a score of 450.

At the other table the American East, playing weak two bids, opened with two diamonds. The bidding continued:

South	*West*	*North*	*East*
Belladonna		Avarelli	
—	—	—	2 ◇
dble	No	3 ◇	No
3 ♠	No	4 ♣	No
4 ♡ (!)	No	5 ◇	No
5NT	No	6 ♡	No
No	No		

When his partner bid four clubs over three spades Belladonna seems to have concluded that if North lacked spade support he must have length in hearts. North's five diamonds was an asking bid and 5NT showed first-round control.

There they were, in the worst of three suits, but the contract proved to be unbeatable. Belladonna won the diamond lead, cashed the ace of spades, and led the top clubs. To prevent a diamond discard, East ruffed the third club with the 10 of hearts. Giorgio overruffed, discarded a diamond from dummy on the king of spades, then led the 8 of hearts and ran it. *Finito la musica!*

In the early days of Italian supremacy the country's most famous player was Eugenio Chiaradia, the Professor (he really was), who returned to his home country, Brazil, after winning the world championship six times. He did not find the winning line on this deal from the 1963 world championship, but he was the first to point it out.

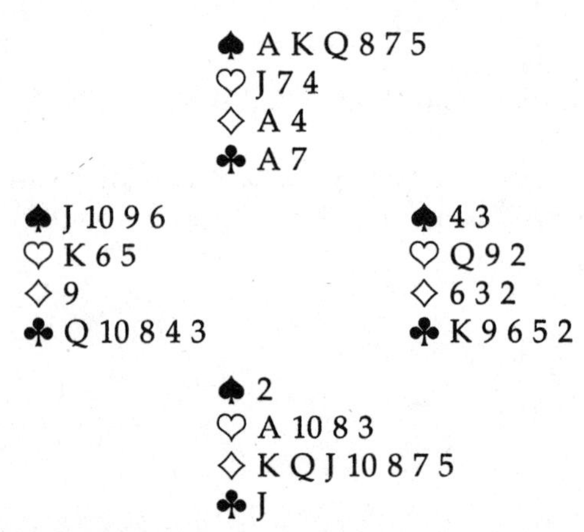

This was the bidding when Italy was North–South:

South	*West*	*North*	*East*
Chiaradia	Théron	Garozzo	Desrousseaux
—	—	—	No
1 ♡(1)	No	2 ♠	No
3 ◇	No	3 ♠	No
4NT(2)	No	5 ♠	No
5NT	No	6 ◇	No
7 ◇(3)	No	No	No

(1) Following the *canapé* style, in which the shorter suit is named first.

(2) Blackwood. It is evident that partner's forcing response of two spades signified a good hand with a strong suit.

(3) He knows that partner holds three aces and good spades. The grand slam seems a fair proposition.

The contract would have been easy had West not made the good lead of a club. He knew the declarer would need to ruff a spade to establish the suit and hoped that the club lead would drive out an important entry.

Two fairly obvious lines of play suggest themselves. One is to cash the ace of spades and ruff a spade, then hope that the trumps will be 2–2 (in itself a better chance than to find the spades 3–3). The other possibility is to play out all the trumps, winning if the spades are 3–3 or if the player with the long spades holds both heart honours.

The Professor played for the first line and was defeated when the diamonds broke 3–1. It looks on the surface as though the squeeze would fail too, as the heart honours are divided, but observe the position after ace of clubs and five rounds of diamonds:

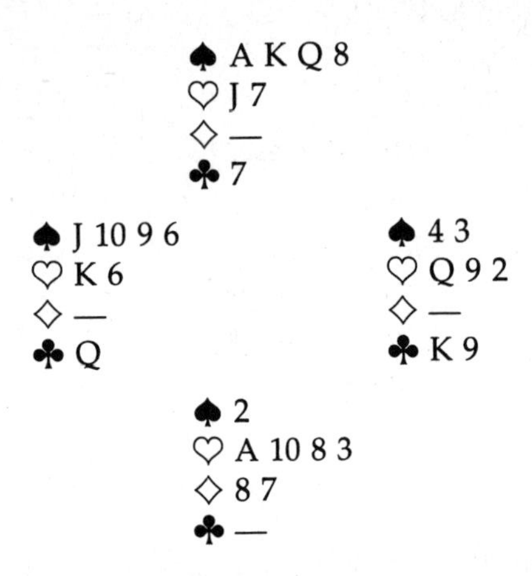

On the 8 of diamonds West can afford a heart and the jack of hearts is thrown from dummy. When the last trump is played West must keep the king of hearts to protect his partner from the finesse, so must release the queen of clubs. Now dummy throws a spade and on three rounds of spades East is squeezed in hearts and clubs. It is the rare 'guard squeeze'.

At the other table the French South opened with a transfer bid of three clubs, and North jumped to four spades, where they rested. This unambitious effort at least resulted in a plus score.

XXIV

When two players as famous as Benito Garozzo and Martin Hoffman are in opposition, you must expect the sparks to fly. On the occasion described here the Italian champion was successful —not that there was anything his opponent could do about it. I will show you first the dummy and the West hand:

♠ Q 8 7 4
♡ J
◇ A Q 10 2
♣ 7 6 4 2

♠ —
♡ A 9 8 7 6
◇ K J 8 7
♣ K Q J 3

In the course of a match played in Manchester the bidding went:

South	*West*	*North*	*East*
Hoffman	Garozzo	Hackett	Sharif
—	—	—	2 ♠
3 ♡	dble	No	No
No			

The opening two spades was weak, showing in principle a six-card suit and about 7–10 points.

Most players would lead the king of clubs as West, but on such occasions it is not, as a rule, good policy to give the declarer a chance to make small trumps by ruffing. Accordingly, Benito led the 7 of hearts, to which all followed. The declarer led a club from dummy, which was covered by the 5, 9 and queen. As West, what would you do now?

Don't tell me—I think I know. You would read the declarer for A 9 and would return a low club to the ace. Let's see what that would have led to.

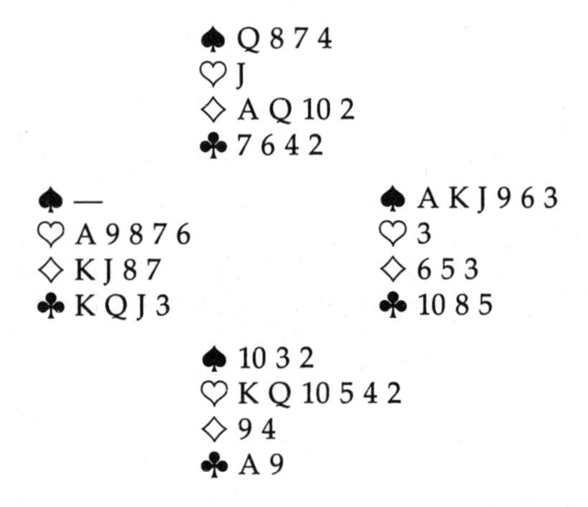

The play has begun: heart to the jack, club to the 9 and queen, club back to the ace. South now finesses the 10 of diamonds, ruffs a club, makes two more diamonds and ruffs another club (or diamond); that is seven tricks and the K Q 10 of hearts will be worth two more.

So you see, a club is not the best return at trick three. Instead, my brilliant partner led the king of diamonds! This makes a crucial difference to the timing. The clubs are blocked for the moment and the best that South can do is make eight tricks by way of diamond ace, club to ace, diamond 10, diamond queen, club ruff, with just two trump tricks to follow.

Garozzo likes to tell the story of one of his rare failures. This was the deal:

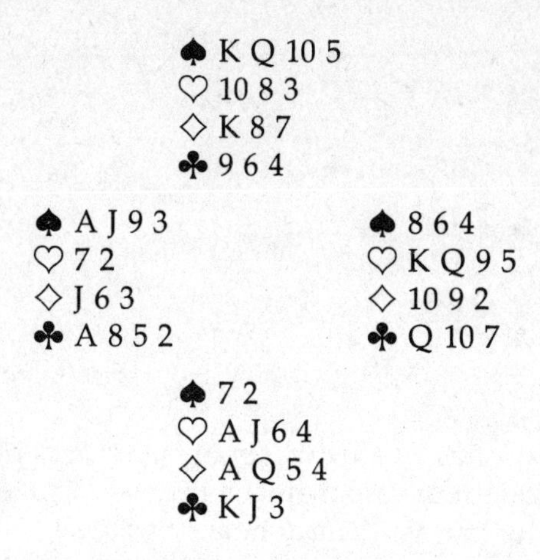

Two elderly ladies occupied the East–West positions and Benito anticipated two good results in a pairs event. But you should never judge by appearances. After a flat first board Benito found himself in 1NT. West led a low diamond to the 9 and ace. South played a spade to the queen and led a heart from the table, on which East played the queen. On the next spade West contributed the *jack*. Expecting to find West with A J x, Garozzo won in dummy and returned a low spade to West's 9.

South had discarded a heart on the third spade, and the discard on the fourth spade was awkward. Finally, he threw another heart. West promptly led a low club to the queen and king. South cashed his winning diamonds now, but on the fourth round he had to throw a club from dummy. When East came in with the king of hearts she led the 10 of clubs, pinning dummy's 9, and Benito finished with just eight tricks, for a very poor score. A master of deceptive play himself, he was the first to congratulate West on her puzzling jack of spades. He who lives by the sword dies by the sword....

While we are on the subject of misplays, you may like to look at a very instructive deal that occurred during the team event at Monte Carlo in 1973. Vivaldi was West and Belladonna East. These were the hands of West and North:

South, who has opened a strong notrump, plays in 3NT, having denied a four-card major on the way. You lead the queen of hearts, your partner (Belladonna) plays the 4, and South wins with the king. He leads a low diamond, probably from A K x x, so you go in with the queen. Partner plays the 10, which you read as a request for spades. You lead the 5 of spades, partner wins with the ace and returns a spade, but now partner's hand is dead. It wasn't easy for him to duck with A x x x, because you might have held Q x x. When in with the queen of diamonds you should have led the *king* of spades, as Vivaldi immediately recognized.

This was a famous Belladonna hand, played against Indonesia in the Bermuda Bowl:

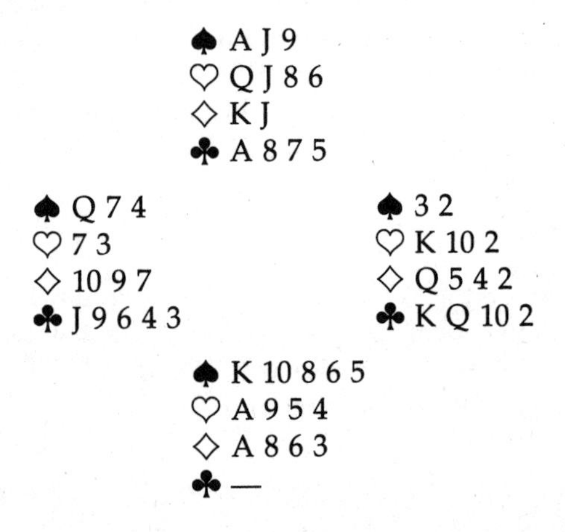

Garozzo, North, opened with a conventional one club, indicating upwards of 16 points. The bidding continued:

South	*West*	*North*	*East*
Belladonna	Moniaga	Garozzo	Karamay
—	—	1 ♣	No
1 ♠	No	3 ♠	No
4 ♣	No	4 ♢	No
4 ♡	No	4 ♠	No
5 ♣	No	5 ♡	No
6 ♢	No	6 ♠	No
No	No		

The final contract was not unreasonable, but the bridgerama commentators, and no doubt the entire audience, were puzzled—amused—by Garozzo's energetic bidding after his very minimum one club opening. Raise to three spades? Cue-bids in diamonds and hearts, causing South to make a grand slam try?

But Benito, on this occasion, was blameless. I had myself joined in a discussion with Garozzo and Belladonna about the meaning of the sequence, one club—one spade—three spades, in 'Super-Precision'. We had agreed that the raise to three spades should signify 'minimum opening and just three trumps'. This was in accordance with the style known in Britain as the 'Principle of Fast Arrival'. With a more promising hand the opener would raise to two spades only, initiating a sequence of asking bids. Having limited his hand, Garozzo was fully entitled to show his controls later. The bid of five hearts was particularly interesting. With a control in hearts he would have bid 4NT over four hearts; the delayed bid of five hearts expressed his holding exactly.

West led the 7 of hearts against six spades. After a double-take when he saw the dummy, Giorgio disposed of the play in less than a minute: two rounds of hearts, ace of clubs and club ruff, three rounds of diamonds, club ruff, leading to:

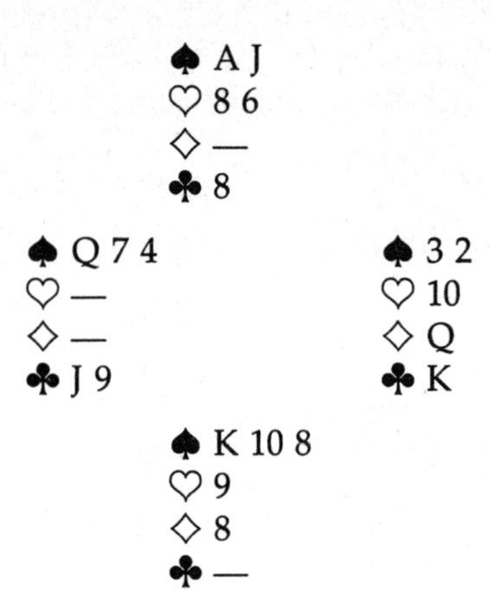

Now a diamond was ruffed, the ace of spades was cashed, and a club was ruffed with the 10 of spades. The king of spades took the twelfth trick, while the queen of trumps and the winning heart fell together at the finish.

XXV

I very much enjoy playing bridge in England. Whenever possible, I have played in the *Sunday Times* Invitation Pairs, an event conducted with a style found nowhere else in the world.* One partnership I have encountered there is that of Rob Sheehan and Irving Rose. Two famous hands of theirs follow.

* As a result of what is euphemistically called an industrial dispute, the *Sunday Times* went out of circulation for eleven months. The tournament was taken over by the magazine *Now!* When *Now!*, in the harsh economic climate, became *Then!*, the tournament was discontinued. A pity, but it had become an enormously expensive promotion. T.R.

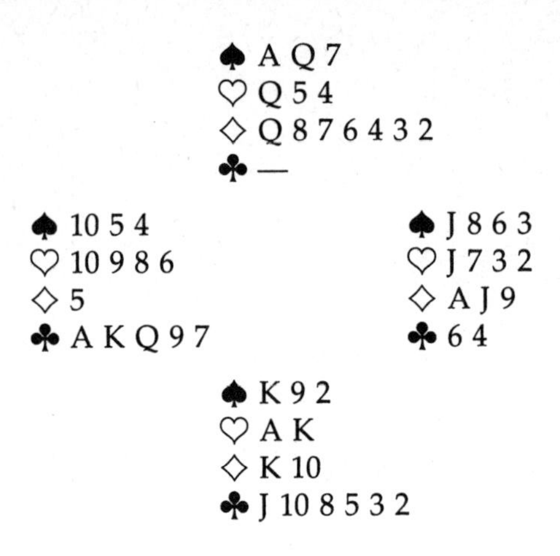

The bidding went:

South	*North*
Rose	Sheehan
—	1 ♢
2 ♣	2 ♢
3NT	No

West led the ace of clubs and switched to the 10 of hearts. Rose crossed to the queen of spades, led a low diamond and finessed the 10!

Why? Because West had led a club into the suit bid by declarer and was certain to be long in the suit. The 10 of diamonds might have lost to a singleton jack, but let's not think of that!

The king of diamonds held the next trick, and Rose then made another surprising play: he led the jack of clubs from hand. West won and led a second heart. Irving now played king and another spade, then exited with a diamond. East cashed his winning spade and had to give dummy the lead in hearts.

On another occasion Rose and Sheehan were opposed to their compatriots, Flint and Cansino, whose bidding on this occasion was a trifle too free.

♠ A Q 3
♡ A 9 8
◇ 8 7 5 2
♣ A J 6

♠ J 5	♠ K 9 8 7 6 2
♡ 6 2	♡ 5
◇ J 6 4 3	◇ K Q 10 9
♣ K 10 7 5 3	♣ 4 2

♠ 10 4
♡ K Q J 10 7 4 3
◇ A
♣ Q 9 8

Rose opened with a multi-coloured two diamonds, which in this instance was equivalent to a weak two in spades. The bidding continued:

South	*West*	*North*	*East*
Flint	Sheehan	Cansino	Rose
—	—	—	2 ◇
4 ♡	No	4NT	No
5 ◇	No	5NT	No
7 ♡	No	No	No

When South showed one ace over 4NT Cansino bid 5NT to confirm that all the aces were held and to suggest a possible grand slam. Whether Flint, having already jumped to four hearts, had enough to justify the grand slam bid seems doubtful to me.

West led the jack of spades and prospects must have seemed poor to the declarer. However, Flint made a fine try by going up with the ace of spades and leading a low spade from dummy at trick two.

East was very much on the spot, because his partner could easily have held J 10 x in spades. After some thought Rose played low and Flint had surmounted the first hurdle. He had three chances now: to play West for king and 10 of clubs; to drop a doubleton 10 of clubs in the East hand; or to squeeze West in diamonds and clubs.

The first move in any case was to lead a heart to the 9, cash ace of diamonds and return to dummy twice to take two more diamond ruffs. After further trump leads the position became:

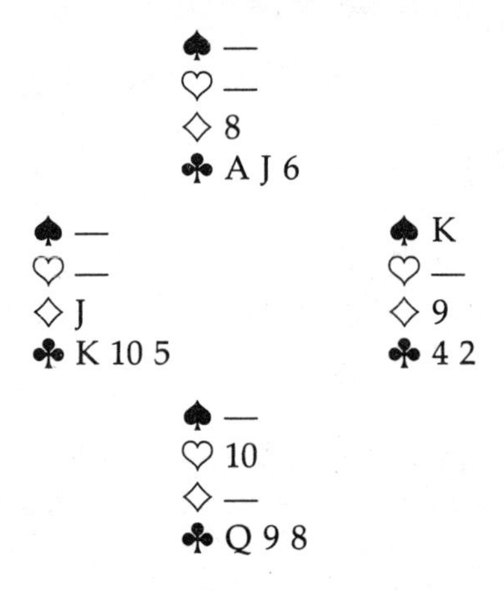

Note that the declarer still had the three options mentioned above. However, Rose had introduced a note of uncertainty by playing the 10, queen and king on the three rounds of diamonds. Had Sheehan played a very deceptive game, keeping two diamonds and two clubs? Reaching this conclusion, Flint played a club to the jack and so lost the contract.

Another British player whom I admire is John Collings, who has long been regarded as one of the finest pairs players in the world. This hand was played quite early in his career, in the European Championship at Ostend.

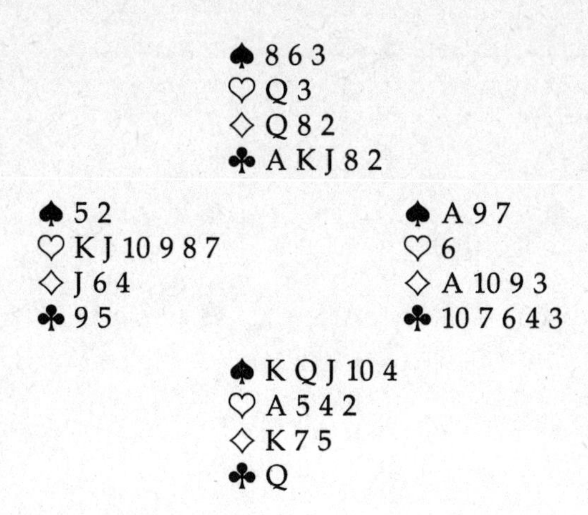

Collings and Cansino bid as follows to the normal contract of four spades:

South	*West*	*North*	*East*
1 ♠	No	2 ♣	No
2 ♡	dble	3 ♠	No
4 ♠	No	No	dble
No	No	No	

West's double of two hearts was quite pointless, simply assisting the declarer to place the cards.

West's lead of the 9 of clubs ran to the queen. The king of spades lost to the ace and East returned his singleton heart. Warned by West's fatuous double, Collings went up with the ace and led a second round of trumps, to which all followed. The position was now:

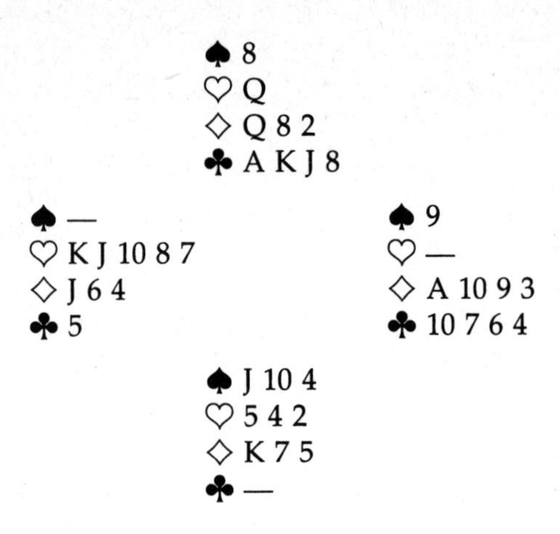

Playing with his usual speed and confidence, John exited with the 4 of spades. East made a trump and the ace of diamonds, but that was all.

XXVI

Your partner opens one heart in fourth position; you respond 2NT and partner gives you 3NT. West leads the 4 of spades and this dummy goes down:

♠ Q 10
♡ A Q J 4
♢ K J 10 6
♣ J 7 5

♠ 4 led

♠ J 8 7
♡ 9 6
♢ A Q 5 4
♣ A 10 9 8

You play the queen of spades from dummy and it holds the trick, East playing the 6. What now?

I have a strong feeling that you would cross to hand with a diamond and take the heart finesse. Mike Lawrence, who at twenty-three was a member of the team that won the world championship in Stockholm in 1970, rested his fortunes on divided honours in clubs, with spades 4–4. Why did he take this line? Because West, remember, had passed in third position. With A K x x x in spades and the king of hearts he would surely have opened. If spades are 4–4, then the combination finesse in clubs presents a better chance of a ninth trick than the single finesse in hearts. Quite easy when you think of it!

One day in the late 1960s I played in a practice game with some Americans who were in training for the world championship. Since it was a friendly game, not an important match, I can bear to confess that my own slightly inaccurate play assisted Bob Hamman to land a most unlikely contract.

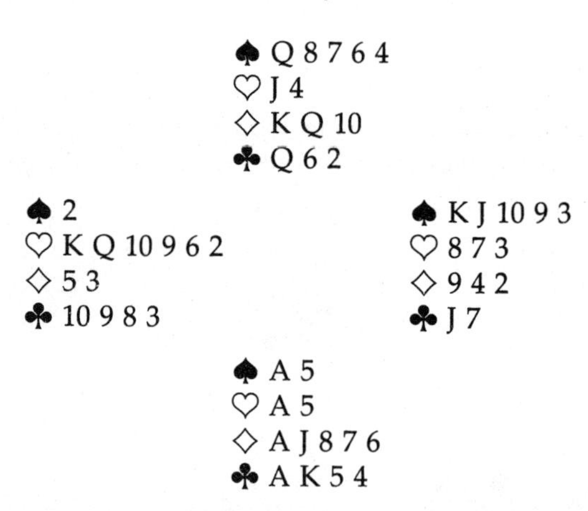

South played in six diamonds after West had made a weak jump overcall of two hearts. I was East and my partner led his singleton spade, which was covered by the 9 and ace. Hamman at once returned a spade, won by my 10. I could have led a heart now, but it seemed reasonable to return a low spade. South ruffed with the jack of diamonds, crossed to dummy with a trump, and ruffed another spade with the ace of diamonds. After a diamond to the queen, he ruffed the fifth spade with his last trump, then crossed to the queen of clubs. The position now was:

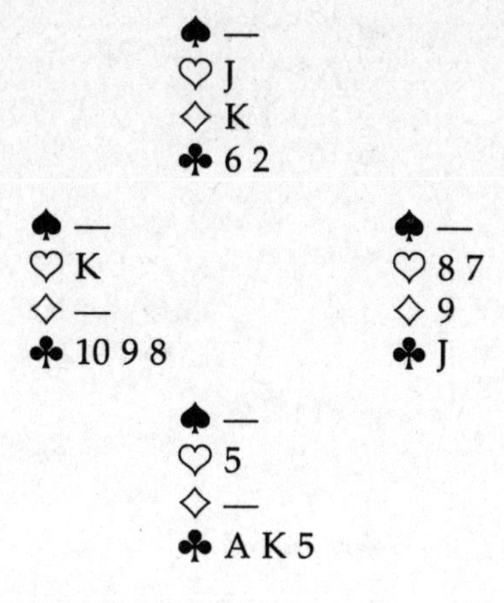

The king of diamonds drew the last trump and on this trick West was squeezed. It wasn't easy to see in advance, but if I had led anything but a spade at trick three the declarer would not have had enough entries to reverse the dummy and squeeze my partner.

You hold in diamonds, a side suit:

◇ K 5 4 2

◇ 10 8 7

West, who has to open up this suit or concede a ruff-and-discard, leads the queen. Because of the play so far, you don't place him with the ace. How would you tackle the suit?

The situation arose when Bobby Wolff was playing against Australia in a world championship match.

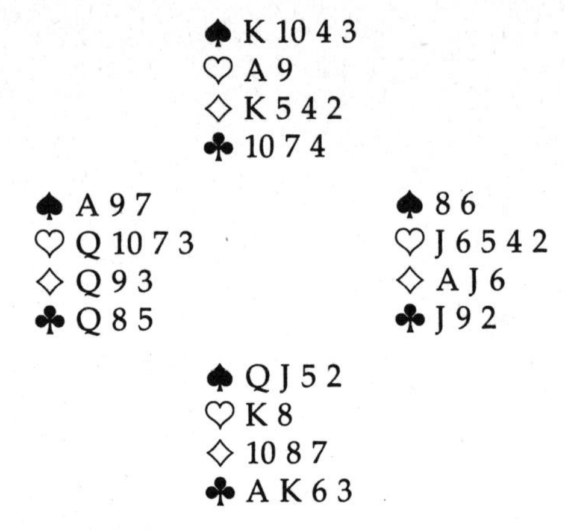

Playing in three spades, South reached this end position and had to avoid losing three tricks in diamonds:

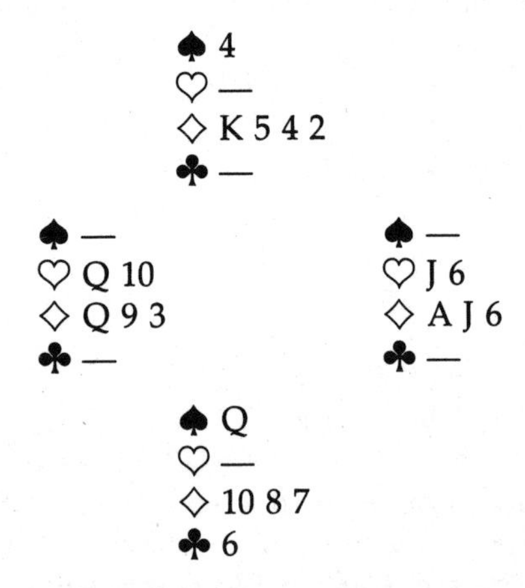

When West leads the queen of diamonds the declarer may seem to be in the midst of a guessing game. Should he cover? If he does, and East returns a low diamond, should he put in the 8 or the 10?

As Bobby realized, the Principle of Restricted Choice applies to this situation. The point is that if West held Q J x he might equally lead the queen or the jack. When he leads the queen there is a presumption that he does not hold the jack. So the best play, and the winning play on this occasion, is to cover the queen with the king and to play the 10 when East returns a low card.

I was unable to be present at Valkenburg, where the French team scored a brilliant success in the 1980 Olympiad, but I was in constant touch with the players over the telephone. This was a celebrated deal between France and Poland:

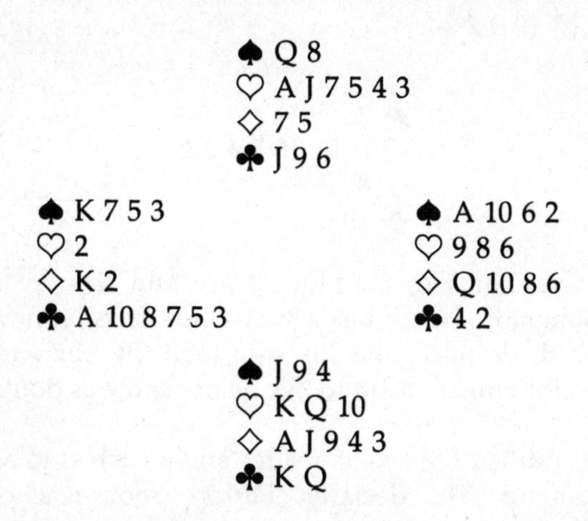

The Polish North opened with a weak two hearts and became declarer in four hearts. The defence was impeccable. East led a club to the ace, a low spade was returned, and East then switched to a diamond, giving the declarer no chance.

At the other table Chemla opened 1NT as South and played in four hearts after a transfer sequence. West began with ace and another club. South won and led a low spade from hand. West, quite naturally, won with the king and switched to the king of diamonds, since from his side it was possible that his partner held the ace. Chemla, very quick-witted as always, played low; thinking he had found the best defence, Kudla led a second diamond and the declarer was able later to dispose of the second spade in dummy.

You will have admired Chemla's play, but have you noticed another very interesting feature? It would have been better play for West to lead a *low* diamond instead of the king.

The following deal is from the match between France and Brazil:

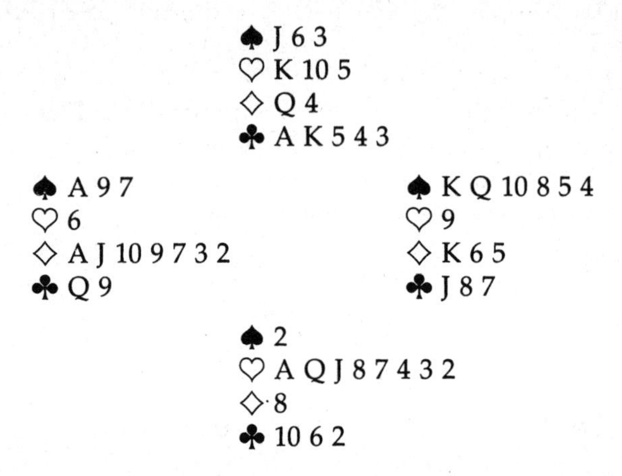

At both tables South opened four hearts and West overcalled with five diamonds. North has a very close decision now. The Brazilian North doubled and his side took the obvious three tricks. Lebel, for France, went to five hearts and was doubled by East.

Chagas, West, led the ace of spades and switched to ace and another diamond. The declarer, Perron, soon reached this ending:

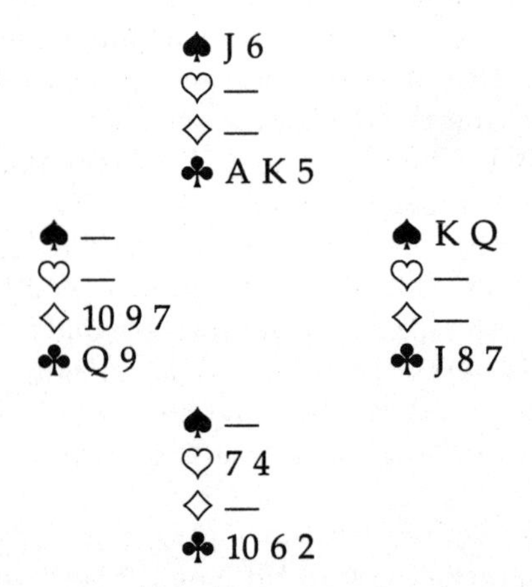

On the next heart a club was thrown from dummy and East was squeezed.

Gabrial Chagas, hero of so many brilliant deals, may seem to have been slightly at fault on this occasion. Either a second spade or a switch to clubs would have defeated the trump squeeze. It is fair to say, however, that from West's angle the declarer might have held two diamonds, and in this case it would have been essential to cash the second trick at once.

Finally, a deal you may have seen before, the celebrated board 52 of the final between France and the United States:

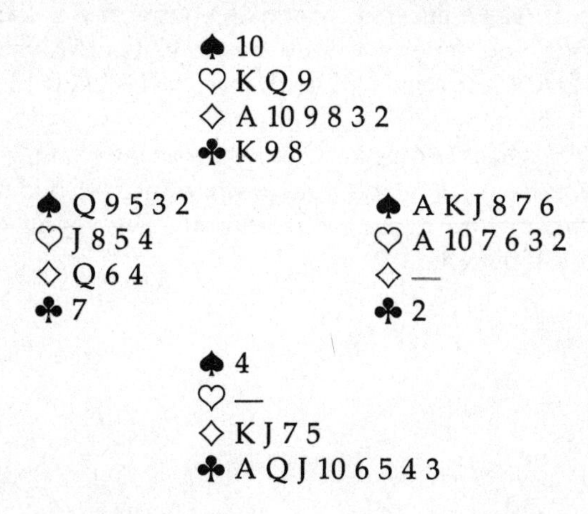

This was the bidding when the French were East–West:

South	*West*	*North*	*East*
Soloway	Perron	Rubin	Lebel
—	No	1 ◇	1 ♠ (!)
2 ♣	4 ♠	No	5 ♣
6 ♣	No	No	6 ♠
dble	No	No	No

The defenders made one heart and one club, for one down. The second table was still more spectacular:

South	*West*	*North*	*East*
Chemla	Wolff	Mari	Hamman
—	No	1 ♢	2 ♢
2 ♡(1)	4 ♠	4NT	5 ♠
6 ♣	No	6 ♢	6 ♠
7 ♢(2)	No	No	dble
No	No	No	

(1) East's two diamonds indicated length in both majors, so two hearts was a cue-bid, promising support for diamonds.

(2) Well, you never know! At this level it is always wise to bid the extra trick, especially when the contract is likely to depend on the lead.

Knowing that his side had considerable length in spades, East laid down the ace of hearts. End of story, for Mari had no problem in picking up the queen of diamonds. The swing of 21 imps decided the match.

XXVII

I have not made money from bridge. That doesn't interest me. I have made money from my work, my profession. When I am successful in a tournament, the thrill lies in the victory, the prize.

Yes, I'm a pushover for cups! Large or small, ornate or plain ugly, I adore them. On show in my drawing-room, they shine with the glamour of success.

My trophies from the cinema are lined up, hidden in corners, lost, objects of little value in my eyes; I have been known to leave them behind in hotel rooms. Yet the smallest bridge cup is a treasure. No matter whether it looks like a funeral urn or a plaque of silver alloy, perched on its block of pseudo-marble, I am proud of it. It is a symbol of my passion for the game. And how can money be a symbol of passion? If there is profit in a game, the pleasure disappears, or nearly so.

Culbertson and Goren made fortunes from bridge, and many others have made a good living, but paradoxically money is far from being the main attraction even for professionals.

If I have made mistakes in my narrative, giving wrong dates and places, it is because I am equally vague about the past and the future. My mind goes blank when I am asked to remember something. When I try to recall thirty feverish years across the green baize, the thousands of hours in a smoky atmosphere, I feel confused.

What a fantastic way it is to spend one's time, playing tens of thousands of deals, hoping all the time to improve one's game!

I am not the best player in the world; I have a long way to go to reach that level. Meanwhile, the best player in the world is improving, too. It is a progression without end. It would be impossible for a bridge player to say one day, 'I've arrived! I can go no further.' Bridge is a game without limits; no one is perfect, and no one ever will be.

As I have said, my head is always swimming with ideas, mostly far removed from the sane, sensible elements of life. It is very important to know how to occupy one's mind. Card games are silly in their way; they contribute little to life. You see, I am becoming a moralist, and I don't like it. I like it so little that I must leave the table where I am writing. It is a sudden change of humour that I cannot explain.

Do not be surprised, my friends. I have warned you about this. I must go up to my room, look at a book or a crossword, or just lie on my bed and think of nothing, dream perhaps. Or run a hot bath and try to relax.

While in the bath, I may think of a proverb that has been repeated for thousands of years in the shadow of the pyramids: 'Throw a lucky man into the Nile and he will emerge with a fish in his mouth.'

Maybe I will come out of my bath with a pack of cards between my teeth.